Creative Programs for Youth and Young Adult Groups

Creative Programs for Youth and Young Adult Groups

Randy Fishell

BAKER BOOK HOUSE
Grand Rapids, Michigan 49516

ISBN: 0-8010-3559-7

Printed in the United States of America

Several Bible versions are quoted: King James Version (KJV); New American Standard
Version (NASB); New International Version (NIV); Revised Standard Version (RSV); New
English Bible (NEB).

Contents

Acknowledgments

Special thanks to Brent Buhler for contributions within these pages, and to Linda Gage, whose affirmation made a difference.

Preface

"He *always* does this," my wife informs those gathered around the Christmas tree. She has ripped approximately a third of the way into the gift-wrapped box I have presented to her and is retrieving items from the package which have no bearing on the gift—old shoes, apples, oranges, rocks. I have used these objects as "filler" to obscure the obvious. Wrapping a record, compact disc, or cassette tape "as-is" would be a dead giveaway; however, creative packaging can guarantee a sense of anticipation.

Similarly, this book is presented in creative packaging. But unlike the filler used in my wife's Christmas presents, the material in this book serves a deeper purpose: to draw young adults closer to Christ. Topics such as self-esteem, risk, friendship, fear, faith, and the purpose of work are treated in a way that challenges and stimulates both thinking Christians and searching hearts.

The book may be used in two ways. Since each full-length program is written for spoken presentation, you may use the text "word-for-word;" practicing aloud prior to the meeting will help to avoid a "canned" delivery. Or, there may be times when you wish only to select from a particular program material which will enhance your own approach to a topic.

The programs may be reasonably tailored to your allotted time frame. If it appears that a program may run overtime, either eliminate one of the activities (usually the last one) or continue the program at the next gathering. If, on the other hand, you need more material to fill some time, simply turn to the "Discussion

Questions" or "Suggested Scripture" section for each program. Both will provide further insight on the topic at hand.

Programs 11–15 are especially suitable for college age/post-high groups but also contain appropriate ideas for mature high school groups.

Best of success as you strive to bring a clear, creative picture of the Christian alternative to young adults.

1

Fear Today, Gone Tomorrow

Purpose

To show that God stands ready to assist us in dealing positively with fear.

Materials Needed

3" X 5" index cards, pencils
White board or newsprint
Cement block and rope (for optional activity "Near Miss")

Preparation

Give a pencil and index card to several group members as they enter. Ask them to write down a time in the past when they feared something which turned out to be harmless. This information will be shared in the activity "Hindfright."

For the optional activity "Near Miss," loop a rope through one end of a cement block and *securely* suspend the assembly from a ceiling beam so that the block hangs at chest level. *Note:* the block must be unobstructed, as it will swing in pendulum fashion.

On the white board or newsprint write down the phobias found in the "Interaction" section. (Cover them, or turn the board around until needed.)

Introduction

Someone has suggested that the two unavoidable things in life are death and taxes. There is something else though that seems inevitable: fear. From the womb to the tomb, this unwelcome emotion pays an occasional visit to every person.

Not all fear is bad; some situations warrant an outpouring of adrenaline. These are rational fears. But at other times feeling afraid is merely a by-product of a skewed perception of reality. When this happens, one's discomfort is the result of an irrational fear. Most of us can probably recall such an instance of unmerited misery.

Activity: "Hindfright"

Ask the previously selected group members to tell about their situations of unwarranted fear. (Allow for others to tell about their fears as time permits.) The experience will help to create an atmosphere of openness; it also points out that irrational fears come in many forms.

Optional Activity: "Near Miss"

This experience demonstrates the reality of irrational fear.

Ask for a male volunteer who is willing to face some potential discomfort. Assure him that he will not be injured. Have the volunteer stand with his heels against a wall. Draw the cement block up to the participant's torso, and inform him that the cement block will be released from that point and allowed to swing back completely. Explain that as long as he stands perfectly still, it is impossible to be hurt by the return swing of the block.

The law of physics does prevent the block from returning beyond the original point of release. But usually, even when this is fully explained, most participants will experience a last-second twinge of discomfort. This is irrational fear.

Interaction

For some individuals, irrational fears can perpetuate into an avoidance pattern. Any situation where the "noxious" stimulus might be encountered is avoided. When this happens, a person is said to have a "phobia."

The term *phobia* may sound threatening to some; it is, however, a common condition. Here are some phobias found in American society: (Reveal the technical names written on the white board. Ask the group members to identify the fear it describes. Then go through the list, asking for responses and supplying definitions as necessary.)

1. Thanatophobia—fear of death
2. Acrophobia—fear of heights
3. Claustrophobia—fear of confining spaces
4. Xenophobia—fear of strangers
5. Agoraphobia—fear of open spaces, or fear of a reaction to fear itself
6. Zoophobia—fear of animals
7. Musophobia—fear of mice
8. Nyctophobia—fear of night or darkness
9. Androphobia—fear of men
10. Gamophobia—fear of marriage

One survey suggests that fear of speaking in public, a form of *lalophobia,* is the most common American phobia. Perhaps two of the less prevalent irrational fears would be *ballistophobia,* fear of missiles, and *chionophobia,* fear of snow. Another fear, one shared by Napoleon Bonaparte and Presidents Herbert Hoover and Calvin Coolidge, is *triskadecaphobia*—fear of the number thirteen. Perhaps Franklin D. Roosevelt forgot that he, too, was a victim of triskadecaphobia when he said, "We have nothing to fear but fear itself."

Bridge

Humans have little trouble finding something to fear. The intensity of fear or anxiety, of course, varies with the perceived threat to our well-being. In a moment, we're going to look at a remedy for fear. But first, let's check some of our reactions to it.

Activity: "Degrees of Dis-ease"

Have group members stand shoulder-to-shoulder in a line. Read the first situation described below. Ask the participants to step forward either one, two, or three paces (three paces being the *most* fear-producing), depending on the degree of fearfulness they believe the situation would produce in them. If the situation would produce little or no fear or anxiety, have those individuals step backward one, two, or three paces, (with three paces being the *least* anxiety-producing). Discuss the responses.

1. The Emergency Broadcast System tone (which signifies a threat of potential disaster in one's area) comes on the radio with no warning or explanation.
2. You have been asked to be the featured guest speaker at your alma mater.
3. An escape has occurred at the nearby state penitentiary. At eleven o'clock that night, you hear what sounds like someone tampering with the lock on your home's back door.
4. You have learned that, due to poor sales, your company is about to make a major announcement concerning layoffs.
5. The morning news informs your city that a package of Happy-O's breakfast cereal from lot #46345 has been found to contain cyanide. You check the box of Happy-O's from which you have just eaten a bowlful. The numbers match.
6. Your telephone rings at 2:00 A.M.
7. The instructor is informing your class that only five persons in a class of seventy students received an "A" on the final exam.
8. At a party, you are awaiting your turn to "tell a little something about yourself" to the group.
9. The "special" person in your life has just informed you that he or she has been diagnosed as having an often-fatal illness.

10. You are going about twenty miles an hour over the speed limit, and looking in your rearview mirror, you realize the car you have just passed is an unmarked state patrol vehicle.

The "Degrees of Dis-ease" experience allows participants to see (literally) that fear is common, and that, depending on how the perceived threat is processed by the individual, the same stimuli can affect each person differently.

Bridge

Fear may have increased in modern society, but the timeless truth found in God's Word can help to conquer it.

Biblical Perspective

One of the great episodes of anxiety recorded in Scripture is found in Matthew 8:23–24 (NIV):

> Then he got into the boat and his disciples followed him. Without warning, a furious storm came up on the lake, so that the waves swept over the boat. But Jesus was sleeping.

The necessary ingredients for fear were present. The disciples were on a sinking ship and their slumbering Savior seemed unconcerned for their safety and his. But Jesus' sleep was interrupted by his distraught friends:

> The disciples went and woke him, saying, "Lord save us! We're going to drown!" He replied, "You of little faith, why are you so afraid?" Then he got up and rebuked the winds and the waves, and it was completely calm. The men were amazed and asked, "What kind of man is this? Even the winds and the waves obey him!" vv. 25–27 (NIV)

The Savior had calmed the sea and the fears of his companions.

Application

The story of Jesus' quieting the storm on Galilee is dramatic. It conveys at least three points that may help ease the sting of fear in our lives:

1. Christians are not immune to fear. The fact that the disciples had a relationship with Jesus did not eliminate their fearful feelings. Similarly for us, simply knowing Christ does not alter basic human perception of danger. But abiding in Christ does make a difference in how we process our fear.
2. Fearlessness is tied to faithfulness. The faith that conquers fear is the result of a consistent relationship with the One who calmed the sea. Placing our trust in him brings a calm assurance and reminds us that we need not face our fears alone.
3. When properly processed, fear becomes soil fertile for personal and spiritual growth. Fear can be the prelude to something amazing. By relying on Christ and facing both rational and irrational fears squarely, one's character will mature. Perhaps greatest of all is that by refusing to give in to fear, one is destined to develop the rare trait of courage.

Wrap-up

It is not God's will that his children live in fear. But in a sin-filled world, even devoted disciples may battle this emotion. The good news is that, even though our faith is weak, Christ is able to calm our waves of fear. His instruments may vary—from the simple encouragement of a friend to professional therapy. But whatever process heaven brings to us for the conquering of our fears, one fact remains: it is ultimately Jesus who brings peace in the midst of our storms.

Discussion Questions

1. Did David feel fear when facing Goliath? Can you recall other godly men and women of the Bible who were afraid? How did they deal with their fear?

2. Explain the differences (if any) between (a) worry, (b) anxiety, and (c) fear.
3. Is fear necessary for human survival? Why/why not? If so, why does Scripture encourage us *not* to be afraid?
4. There is a clinical adage that says, "Face the fear and the fear will disappear." Can you cite any examples from your own experience that this is true?
5. A friend confides in you that he/she is afraid to fly. As a Christian, what specific course of action might you recommend?

Suggested Scripture

Psalm 23:4; Philippians 4:6–7; 1 John 4:18.

For Further Reading

Reuven Bar-Levav, *Thinking in the Shadow of Feelings* (New York: Simon & Schuster, 1988).

Bruce Larson, *Living Beyond Our Fears* (San Francisco: Harper and Row, 1990).

Cecil Osborne, *Release from Fear and Anxiety* (Waco, Tex: Word, 1976).

Ann Seagrave and Faison Covington, *Free from Fears* (New York: Simon & Schuster, 1987).

2
McSpirituality

Purpose

To show that attaining true spirituality requires discipline and commitment.

Materials Needed

White board or newsprint, marker
Bible

Introduction

Pious persons do exist. Each of us can probably recall a modern-day disciple—a church leader, a teacher, a business acquaintance—whose piety has shone through.

Ultimately, the goal of Christianity is holiness, a transforming of the mind and spirit. The process of becoming a spiritual person varies from individual to individual. But the Bible reveals a mindset to be assumed by all who would become more like Christ. Let's have some fun discovering what it is.

Activity: "The Same Game"

Whet the audience's appetite for discovering some "secret ingredients" of spirituality. Read aloud the first grouping listed below. Explain that all of the items (or people, etc.) have something in common; the audience must guess what the common element is. Use the following groupings or create a different set.

1. Dolly
   Mary
   Eleanor
   Betty
   Barbara
   (First Ladies)

2. "The Life of Riley"
   "Dragnet"
   "Gunsmoke"
   "The Lone Ranger"
   "Superman"
   (Radio programs which later became television shows)

3. New York
   Knoxville
   Chicago
   Seattle
   Montreal
   (Cities which have hosted a World's Fair)

4. Harry Truman
   Gerald Ford
   George Bush
   (Left-handed U.S. Presidents)

5. Kangaroo
   Pita bread
   Jeans
   (Things that have pockets)

6. College degree
   Pickle
   Adulthood
   Olympic medal
   Relationship
   (Things that require a period of time to attain, i.e., "delayed fulfillment")

7. Fast food restaurant
   Fax machine
   Sod
   Credit card
   Microwave oven
   (Things that immediately satisfy, or "instant gratification")

To conclude, hold up a Bible and ask the audience to consider (without answering at this point) in which of the final two categories, if either, the Bible and the way of life to which it points belongs.

Bridge

Today human desires are often swiftly satisfied. Even on a leisurely day, lunch may be eaten at a fast-food restaurant, and pictures picked up from a one-hour photo finisher. Later that evening a VCR might be fast-forwarded to see "whodunit" before the scoundrel even has a chance to do it!

There is still, however, one thing which requires time, discipline, and commitment: a deeper relationship with Jesus Christ.

Biblical Perspective

In *Ordering Your Private World,* Gordon MacDonald writes, "If we are ever to develop a spiritual life that gives contentment it will be because we approach spiritual living as a discipline, much as the athlete trains his body for competition."[1]

MacDonald is not the first to suggest that true spirituality requires a consistent training. The apostle Paul's wordbrush paints this picture: "Do you not know that in a race all the runners compete, but only one receives the prize? So run that you may obtain it . . . Every athlete exercises self-control in all things. They do it to receive a perishable wreath, but we an imperishable" (1 Cor. 9:24–25 RSV).

Those to whom Paul wrote were well-seasoned in the world of sports. Corinth was the host city for the Isthmian games, a series of athletic events second only to the Olympic games in renown.

In the original language, the phrase "running a race" is more fully translated "race course." Paul likely had in mind the track in the Corinthian stadium, whose ruins still stand. As for the "perishable wreath," it was a leafy crown made of Isthmian pine. There were no gold, silver, or bronze medals to be awarded but many would give their all to receive this passing symbol of victory. The ancient writer Horace indicated that a candidate for these games "must be pure, sober, enduring, to obey orders, to eat sparely and simply and to bear effort and fatigue for ten months before the contest."

Becoming a champion takes time and effort. Likewise, prize-winning faith requires discipline and commitment. Never will salvation be earned by such effort, but the gift of grace will be more deeply realized by consistently striving to glorify its giver. That is the race to be run and, through him, eventually won.

As Paul's passage implies, there is no viable shortcut to heaven. In a world of quick burgers, there is no "McSpirituality." Similarly, no "spiritual steroids" can achieve what long-term dedication to spiritual discipline can accomplish. That is why Paul in Hebrews 12:1 wrote, ". . . let us run with *perseverance* the race marked out for us." Like a runner who would win the prize, becoming a more devoted disciple takes time—and a commitment to know Christ better. Let's try to produce some collective insight regarding commitment.

Activity: "Ten Commandments of Commitment"

This stimulating activity will help individuals strengthen their life commitments. The specific goal is to encourage commitment to spiritual discipline, but the principles may be applied to achieving any goal.

At random, ask for ten specific suggestions that are likely to help individuals become more committed. Begin each "commandment" with the phrase "Thou shalt . . .", and use King James-style English to finish the sentence(s). Write the commandments on a white board or newsprint. If the audience is stymied, use the following as examples:

1. "Thou shalt know specifically that to which thou art committing." (Focus)
2. "Thou shalt be convinced in thine own mind that thy commitment is worth the price thou wilt be paying." (Belief)
3. "Thou shalt prioritize thy time to achieve the goal to which thou hast committed." (Organization)
4. "Thou shalt ask for divine assistance in staying committed." (Prayer)
5. "Thou shalt make thyself responsible to another for thy commitment." (Accountability)
6. "Thou shalt on occasion place thyself in a situation where thy commitment can be strengthened through practice." (Practical application)

7. "Thou shalt try again when thou failest or falter in thy commitment." (Recommitment)
8. "Thou shalt seek an audience with those who have demonstrated successful commitment." (Counsel)
9. "Thou shalt increase or decrease thy commitments as thy lifestyle and priorities permit." (Growth)
10. "Thou shalt encourage others to experience the joy of commitment." (Outreach)

As each commandment is suggested, ask for an illustration of how the particular precept might be used. The leader may wish to have these suggestions printed, then distributed the following week.

Illustration

Lewis Timberlake, in *It's Always Too Soon to Quit,* tells of a man who made a commitment:

> While attending tiny Campbell College in North Carolina, twenty-three-year-old Orville Peterson worked desperately to win a place on the United States track team. After the first day of the decathlon tryouts, Peterson held a solid eighth place in a field of fifty entrants. However, on the second day of the first event, the 100-meter hurdles, disaster paid a visit. Orville Peterson pulled muscles and ligaments in his left thigh that rendered him virtually immobile.
>
> No one imagined that he could continue with the kind of excruciating pain he must have been enduring. But they were wrong, because Orville Peterson had come to compete. He first refused to see even a trainer for fear he'd be forced to withdraw from the competition. So Orville continued in the next event, the discus throw. While experiencing agonizing pain in his leg, he managed to throw the heavy discus 137 feet, 5 inches. After accomplishing this seemingly impossible feat, he managed to pole vault an amazing 12 feet, 5 inches as well as throw the javelin 206 feet, 9 inches! But these performances, while good under such circumstances, caused him to drop to fourteenth in the standings. Only one event remained on the second day of the competition—

the grueling 1,500 meters—four laps of sheer misery for even the most fit and healthy athlete.

The crack of the start gun broke the heavy silence as spectators watched in eager anticipation, wondering how this brave young man could even make it around the first lap. The fact is, the winner crossed the finish line in just under five minutes with the rest of the field close behind him. The track was empty—except for one lone runner.

Orville Peterson, his left thigh heavily wrapped, had promised himself that he'd complete the decathlon competition—even if he didn't win a place on the American team. In spite of his debilitating injury, he was willing to pay the price to achieve his dream. To do this, Orville had to finish the 1,500 meters, even if it meant he would have to limp the whole way . . . and limp he did.

As the crowd began to cheer Peterson on, his fellow competitors lined the sides of the track and shouted support. Then the strains of the theme from *Chariots of Fire* poured out of the public address loudspeakers, filling the stadium with inspiring music. To Orville, this was bigger and better and meant more than becoming another Carl Lewis, Bruce Jenner, or Mary Decker. It was bigger than signing endorsement contracts for sports equipment or athletic clothing, and better than making public appearances.

As Orville entered the home stretch of his final lap of that painful race and headed for the finish line, the PA announcer quietly read this ancient Greek saying to the listening crowd: "Never ask for victory, ask only for courage. For if you endure the struggle, you bring honor to yourself; but most importantly, you bring honor to us all."

Peterson's time in the 1,500 meters that day was nearly ten minutes, almost twice as long as the winner's time. He earned no points for his effort and dropped to thirty-second place in the final standings. But he had finished the race. And that is why those who were there will testify that Orville Peterson was the biggest winner of all . . .[2]

Wrap-up

Orville Peterson knew the meaning of the words *discipline* and *commitment.* He was determined to finish the course he was running. Similarly, the Christian who would grow in grace must devote time and effort to running the race of discipleship.

There is a race to be run and all who commit to finishing it will one day claim a prize greater than earthly life itself—an eternity with the Savior.

Discussion Questions

1. Define "spiritual discipline." Give some examples of the form(s) it might take in the Christian life.
2. What might be some ingredients of spiritual discipline that are common to everyone?
3. What is the role of grace in the "race for holiness"?
4. Why does Paul say to "run with *perseverance*"? How does the phrase relate to the assurance of one's salvation?
5. Have several individuals tell about a time when commitment (or lack of it) made a difference in his or her life. What one thing was learned about commitment from the experience?

Suggested Scripture

Psalm 1:1–3; Matthew 7:24–27; John 15:1–8; Ephesians 6:10–18.

For Further Reading

Bob Benson, *He Speaks Softly* (Waco, Tex.: Word, 1987).

Jerry Bridges, *Pursuit of Holiness* (Colorado Springs: NavPress, 1978).

Gordon MacDonald, *Ordering Your Private World* (Nashville: Thomas Nelson, 1984).

3

Test of Success

Purpose

To more fully understand the dynamics of true success for the Christian.

Materials Needed

Index cards, pencils
White board or newsprint, marker
Saucepan or basket

Preparation

Letters of alphabet, individually cut
Index cards for "The Wealthy Not-So-Old Politician" activity. (These may be distributed just prior to the beginning of the program for participants to complete.)

Introduction

Success. The subject catches our upwardly mobile interest. And who can blame us? After all, Madison Avenue has made it clear that maximum fulfillment awaits those who achieve "success." It is the Land of Oz at the end of the corporate yellow brick road. We're taught to savor its flavor and dress to gain its favor. And slowly, almost imperceptibly, success becomes the heady object of our affections. We no longer merely *want* to make it to the top, we *need* to succeed.

When it comes to those who've "made it" in the eyes of the world, Scripture has painted some intriguing portraits. The lifestyles of both the rich and famous and the poor and not-so-well-known find affirmation. Is this some kind of biblical paradox par excellence? Or is it possible there is something waiting to be discovered that can help ease the tension? The first step in successfully solving this puzzle is to define more clearly what we mean by this thing called *success*.

Activity: "Success Soup"

Place cut-up letters of the alphabet in a basket or saucepan. (If the twenty-six letters of the alphabet are less than the typical group turnout, supply duplicates as necessary.) Pass the pan around, and have every group member select one letter each. Each participant is to think of an attribute necessary for success that begins with the chosen letter. For example, if the letter "D" was selected, that individual might suggest the word *dedication*. Allow a moment or two for consideration, then go around the room, asking each person to tell his or her response. These are written on the white board or newsprint. Do not embarrass anyone who is unable to supply a response. Instead, ask for the group to assist. Also, allow words which begin with a similar *sound*, such as "excellence" for the letter "X."

"Success Soup" furnishes specific, helpful information concerning what it takes to be a "success." Additionally, it serves as a lead-in to the next program segment.

Bridge

The recipe for success contains many ingredients. But attributes fostered outside of the Christian framework, while leading to earthly success, are destined to bring ultimate failure. Jesus made this very clear in an encounter long ago. Hopefully, it will come into even greater focus today and help us discover the secret of true success. The names and places may have changed, but the message remains the same.

Activity: "The Wealthy Not-So-Old Politician"

Ask for volunteers willing to serve as subjects in a good-spirited experiment that will present a scriptural perspective on priorities and eternal success. Distribute to the volunteers the set of previously prepared index cards on which you have written the following:

1. Please write the name of a nearby town: _____.
2. Please write your first name: _____.
3. Please write the name of a local fast-food restaurant: _____.
4. Please write the name of a local discount store: _____.
5. Please write your occupation: _____.
6. Please write your first name: _____.
7. Please write your first name: _____.
8. Please write the kind of car you drive: _____.
9. Please write your last name: _____.
10. Please write the name of a nearby town: _____.

Ask the volunteers to fill in the blanks; then collect the cards, arranging them in numerical order. Finally, read aloud the story below, inserting the response contained on the index card that corresponds with the number in the script.

The Wealthy Not-So-Old Politician

Once upon a time, in the not-so-faraway city of _1_, there lived a wealthy not-so-old politician named _2_. Now _2_'s life was filled to overflowing with the material benefits his/her station in life afforded him/her. Any evening, on a mere whim, dinner would be catered by _3_. The latest sound system from _4_ was just another symbol of the status he/she had attained.

Concerning the specifics of his/her political office, _2_ held the powerful position of _5_ for the bustling metropolis of _1_. As such, there was little in the area of amenities that _2_'s occupation could not provide.

Ironically, however, a feeling of discontentment haunted _2_. It was as if, somewhere in the hidden recesses of his/her mind, _2_ knew that the *ultimate* success was yet to appear. Defining the elusive entity, along with a plan for seizing it, continued to evade the savvy and prowess of _2_'s upwardly mobile mind.

One morning, as he/she sat reading the _1_ *Times,* the telephone rang. It was _6_, _2_'s personal advisor.

"Did you happen to catch the ad on page seven of today's *Times?*" _6_ inquired. "It appears that yet another scam has found its way to our fair district."

Suddenly very curious, _2_ quickly flipped through the pages until he/she came to the ad. It read: "Sign Up Now for the Ultimate Success Seminar Sponsored by Eternal Returns, Inc. To register, call 1-(800)-FOR LIFE."

"So, would you like me to pursue an investigation?" _6_ asked shortly.

_2_ paused, but finally replied, "Uh, no. I'll check into this myself." With that, the wealthy not-so-old politician hung up and then quickly dialed the number featured in the ad.

A pleasant voice came on the line: "Hello, my name is _7_; thank you for calling the Ultimate Success Seminar number. Would you like to register now?"

"Yes, I would," _2_ replied. This was not to be an undercover maneuver aimed at exposing a potential con game. Rather, the wealthy not-so-old politician hoped to discover the missing link in his/her chain of achievement. So the following Tuesday night _2_ pulled up to the seminar site in his/her _8_ limousine, stepped out, and walked into the lobby of the _9_ Hotel and Convention Center.

_2_ had a plan. The Ultimate Success Seminar was scheduled to meet over a period of several weeks. But this wealthy not-so-old politician was a busy person and could not afford to wait that long. After the evening's presentation, he/she would personally confront the presenter. If he were truly a master teacher, as the ad suggested, surely he could quickly furnish the information _2_ needed.

The instructor proved to be persuasive yet gentle. It was obvious that he believed deeply in what he was saying. All told, by the end of the evening, _2_ was convinced that this teacher did indeed hold the key that could unlock the door to ultimate success. But winners need specific advice from their coach. Accordingly, _2_ inched toward the lectern, cleared his/her throat, then spoke. "My good man," _2_ began, assuming an air of confidence, "while your stories are captivating, I question the expedience of your method."

The teacher's gaze fell on his student and signaled that _2_ had gained his/her mentor's full attention. The wealthy not-so-old politician got to the point. "What I would like to know is what I must do to attain the ultimate success."

The teacher, apparently sensing the status of his questioner, replied, "Surely you already know the ten basic rules of success. Fact is," he added, pointing to the book _2_ held, "you'll find them in the first portion of your training manual."

"These rules," _2_ responded, holding up the manual, "are ancient history. Why, I've been following them since my days back at _7_ middle school. So, how about it? What's the *real* kicker to the big time?"

The teacher paused. He then spoke in caring yet convicting tones. "You lack one thing," he informed _2_ . "Go, forfeit your power and prestige; then come, and follow me."

A shocked look on _2_'s face soon turned to disappointment. The teacher watched with hurt in his eyes as the wealthy not-so-old politician silently walked away. Several associate instructors now gathered around the teacher, apparently awaiting a response regarding the incident. It soon came.

"How hard it will be for those who are driven by achievement to pass the test of ultimate success." Then, turning to his colleagues, he finished by saying, "For many that are first will be last; and many that 'fail' will succeed."

Bridge

By now it should be clear that the preceding tale is based on the biblical story of the rich young ruler. While the real rich young ruler requested how to obtain eternal life, the story also reveals the principles of true "success."

Biblical Perspective

The story of the rich young ruler is found in the tenth chapter of Mark. Here was a man who apparently had it all: wealth, power, prestige, and an ethical record that neared perfection. Here was success personified.

Jesus' eyes, as usual, were not fixed on the outward appearance, but rather on this man's heart. Beginning with Mark 10:17, we see the Master purposefully leading the rich young ruler to a point of spiritual discomfort:

> As Jesus started on his way, a man ran up to him and fell on his knees before him. "Good teacher," he asked, "what must I do to inherit eternal life?"
>
> "Why do you call me good?" Jesus answered. "No one is good—except God alone. You know the commandments: 'Do not murder, do not commit adultery, do not steal, do not give false testimony, do not defraud, honor your father and mother.'"
>
> "Teacher," he declared, "all these things I have kept since I was a boy."
>
> Jesus looked at him and loved him. "One thing you lack," he said. "Go, sell everything you have and give to the poor, and you will have treasure in heaven. Then come, follow me."
>
> At this the man's face fell. He went away sad, because he had great wealth. (NIV)

Ancient ruler or modern disciple—this story contains not only the secret of salvation, but also the answer for all who would pass the test of true success. Its discovery is worth pursuing.

Activity Discussion

Divide the participants into four groups. Each group is to briefly discuss the following question: What was missing in his "lifenotes" that caused the rich, young ruler to fail his "test of success"? Suggest that reading the remainder of the biblical passage (Mark 10:23–30) may prove helpful.

After a few minutes, have each group reduce their conclusion to five words or less and then tell other groups their findings. List these responses on the white board or newsprint. Ask these questions about the responses: For the Christian, can these things and the pursuit of *earthly* success conscionably coexist? If not, why not? And if so, how? Ask for specific examples.

Wrap-up

For the Christian, true success ultimately demands a radical, Spirit-driven reorientation. It means choosing to focus on the things of eternity instead of earthly things.

Jon Johnston has suggested that one way to help maintain a godly perspective in this matter is to pursue excellence instead of success. He contrasts the two concepts when he writes,

> Success offers a hoped-for goal.
> Excellence provides a striven-for standard.
>
> Success bases our worth on a comparison to others.
> Excellence gauges our value by measuring us against our own potential.
>
> Success grants its rewards to the few, but is the dream of multitudes.
> Excellence is available to all living beings, but is accepted by the special few.
>
> Success focuses its attention on the external—becoming the tastemaker for the insatiable appetites of the conspicuous consumer.
> Excellence beams its spotlight on the internal spirit—becoming the quiet, but pervasive, conscience of the conscientious who yearn for integrity.
>
> Excellence cultivates principles and consistency, which ensure that we will treat all persons as intrinsically valuable ends—the apex of our heavenly Father's creation.[1]

For the Christian, success means living our lives on earth as citizens of the kingdom of heaven. This is an excellent, indeed, the only way to pass eternity's "test of success."

Discussion Questions

1. Is the pursuit of success ever a viable option for the Christian? If so, under what circumstances?
2. Proverbs 16:3 says, "Commit to the LORD whatever you do, and your plans will succeed." What does this mean?
3. What are some reasons an individual may come to love success?
4. How can the Christian know that his or her priorities regarding achievement reflect God's will?
5. Winston Churchill once said: "Success is never final, failure is never fatal; it is courage that counts." As a Christian, do you agree or disagree with this statement? What else "counts"?

Suggested Scripture

Proverbs 16:3; Matthew 6:19–21; Mark 8:36; Hebrews 12:1–2a.

For Further Reading

Randy Alcorn, *Money, Possessions and Eternity* (Wheaton, Ill.: Tyndale House, 1989).

Anthony Campolo, *Who Switched the Price Tags?* (Waco, Tex.: Word, 1987).

Jon Johnston, *Christian Excellence: Alternative to Success* (Grand Rapids: Baker Book House, 1985).

Cecil Murphey, *Another Chance* (Philadelphia: The Westminster Press, 1987). Appendix D, "Life Values," pp. 125–130 is a group activity on life priorities.

Stacy and Paula Rinehart, *Living for What Really Matters,* (Colorado Springs: NavPress, 1987).

4

Reflections of the Divine

Purpose

To affirm the intrinsic worth of each individual as an image-bearer of God.

Materials Needed

Paper, pencils for all
White board or newsprint, marker

Preparation

None

Introduction

In the world of collectibles, two of the factors that determine an object's value are scarcity and demand. Antique furniture, wind-up toys, 78 rpm records—certain of these and more have become items of value. An example of a treasured collectible is a Queen Anne bureau bookcase that sold for a whopping $860,000! Of course, there's also the antique golf ball that someone took home for $1,790. Or how about the 1931 Packard pedal car toy that fetched $5,700? And would you believe a 1918 U.S. airmail invert error stamp went for $135,000? That price tag makes the $12,000 paid for Judy Garland's *Wizard of Oz* slippers look like a steal!

All of us wish we owned at least one object of great value. But what many of us fail to realize is that we already possess something worth more than all the previous combined—our own unique personhood. As to our rarity, each of us is a "one-of-a-kind." And demand? There was One who was willing to give his very life so that he might claim us for his own.

So many individuals go through life unaware of their real value, convinced that they are worthless. If only these people could realize their true worth as a child of God, their lives would be favorably changed forever.

A sense of low self-esteem is devastating, both *inter*personally and *intra*personally. When someone perceives, either consciously or subconsciously, that he or she is a "nobody," the natural reaction is self-contempt. After all, no one likes a loser. Accordingly, self becomes something either to be altered or avoided altogether. Cosmetic surgery, drugs, or intense busyness are typical choices for alteration and avoidance. But for others the ultimate solution lies not in avoidance or alteration, but in self-eradication—suicide.

A poor self-image is usually communicated to others either in the form of egotism, which is really insecurity in disguise, or its opposite, self-belittlement and super-humility.

Developing a healthy sense of self-worth is a requirement for achieving more positive life experiences. Happily, as we'll discover, the Christian has a decided advantage in developing self-esteem. Nevertheless, some Christians encounter barriers to self-worth.

Bridge

In his book *You're Someone Special,* Dr. Bruce Narramore describes an activity that he uses in self-esteem seminars. Borrowing his concept may help us begin to expose some barriers to self-esteem.

Activity: "Pictures of Humility"

Distribute pencil and paper to all participants. Ask them to write down the name of the individual whom they consider to be the most humble person they have ever met. They are then to write down the two words that best describe that person (i.e., "gentle," "loving," etc.). When they have finished, ask participants to reveal their "nomination" and the two words they have chosen to describe that individual. Write these on the white board or newsprint.

Typically, the resulting compilation will contain mostly words that conjure up images of exceeding mild-manneredness, such as "quiet" and "reserved." What will be glaringly absent are words which fit a more outgoing and assertive personality style, such as "dynamic" or "enthusiastic."

The purpose of "Pictures of Humility" is to show the prevailing attitude that sees humility as a lackluster trait and, concurrently, how that affects self-esteem.

Application

As we've seen, the term *humility* evokes a rather specific image in many minds. But as Bruce Narramore writes, ". . . humility is not passivity. The truly humble person is confident of both his strengths and his rights. With his strength, he can choose to take a position of service or suffering, if that is called for. Because of his inner strength, he can also rise up and aggressively combat evil when circumstances call for action."[1]

True humility is not simply assuming a lowly attitude. Rather, it is acknowledging dependency on God, regardless of personality traits.

It is true that the Christian is called to maintain a sacrificial attitude. Since for some this translates into a lifestyle of self-suppression, "true humility" is seen as being incongruent with self-affirmation. The sad result of this skewed view of humility is that the very environment in which self-esteem might grow becomes a desert of unnecessary self-denial. Only by understanding what true humility is (and is not) can such a person begin to build a proper sense of self-worth.

A misconception of humility is one blockade to building self-esteem. But there are many other deterrents on the road to achieving a sense of self-worth. Here are a few (list on white board or newsprint):

Negative parental feedback

For many of us, the most important element in the formation of self-worth is the picture provided by our parents. If ours was a positive experience, we had a greater chance of feeling good about ourselves in later life. But if it was a negative relationship, our self-esteem probably suffered.

As either parents or persons who may be a child's "significant other," it's important to be aware of how we might be subtly undermining that child's self-esteem. Some of these ways include:

1. *Conditional love.* Some parents act as if their love for a child depends on performance or a set of rules and conditions. The child learns that outside such circumstances he is "unloved." It's hard to love one's self unconditionally when the concept is foreign to one's home experiences.
2. *Discounting.* Similar to conditional love, this is the conscious or subconscious practice of never giving total affirmation. If the recital piece was 99 percent perfect, the parent may at first laud the effort but eventually will get around to mentioning the 1 percent imperfection. After a childhood filled with such discounts, it's easy to see how a general sense of inadequacy would develop.
3. *Unempathic bonding.* Some individuals have a bent toward impassive "Stoicism." Males in particular seem to have a difficult time showing affection. A child is not overtly *taught* that he is not cared about by the withholding of affection. But the message is inevitably *caught.* Again, the negative effects on self-esteem can be lifelong.
4. *Separation and/or divorce.* Psychologists tell us that children tend to assume responsibility for their parent's marital conflicts. "If only I were a better son (or daughter), Mom and Dad would still be together" is their unconscious line

of reasoning. Obviously, they cannot love themselves if they feel they are "to blame" for their parents' pain.

Peer rejection

Another key ingredient in forming self-esteem is the way we're treated by our peers. Short neck, long legs, high forehead, low I.Q.—all can become targets of ridicule. Ironically, those who belittle others usually harbor a poor self-image themselves. Only if "significant others" furnish massive doses of unconditional love to those so unkindly treated will the victims understand that they are valued for their personhood, *period.*

Perfectionism

The perfectionistic individual is the person who is continually setting unrealistic goals for himself. Naturally, when the goal isn't reached, those people feel like failures, and tell themselves that they "should've done better." Such people are obviously trapped on a no-win treadmill. It's also easy to see that under these kind of circumstances there is little place for self-esteem. The only solution is to realize where the pressure is really coming from— within—then either modify what was an impossible goal or grant permission to others to help share the load.

Guilt

Still another barrier to achieving self-esteem is guilt—false or genuine. Often, when people deliberately focus on guilt feelings, it's because they are subconsciously punishing themselves. Forgiveness just doesn't seem to fit the crime. Accordingly, feeling good about oneself is simply not allowed. Remembering the grace of God is the only thing that can set the guilt-ridden person free.

Excessive competitiveness

A final stumbling block on the road to self-worth is an exaggerated sense of competition. In any contest, if someone wins, another must lose; if there is a first, there is also a last. This arrangement works wonders for those who come out on top. But self-esteem can take a beating in the person on the bottom.

For better or for worse, competition is here to stay. Fortunately, so is God's church. And there's no better place to affirm each other on the basis of who a person is, rather than what he did during the week.

(At this point, solicit from the audience other barriers to self-esteem.)

We've mentioned a few of the many ways that a person's self-esteem can be hindered from growing in a sin-filled world. Psychologists and others could undoubtedly supply more. But Scripture contains an incredible, undeniable fact that can help turn even the poorest self-image around.

Biblical Perspective

A person's self-worth is rooted in creation itself. Reaching the end of that first week of human history, God capped it off by creating humanity. But perhaps the most amazing fact of this creative act is that he patterned us after divinity itself! In Genesis 1:26–27 we read: "Then God said, 'Let us make man in our image, in our likeness' . . . So God created man in his own image, in the image of God he created him; male and female he created them."

We are designed as a reflection of the divine! Certainly we are not like God in every aspect, yet we must not deny our heavenly heritage.

Nothing can destroy the reality of our inherent self-worth. It is true that some individuals will not be able to make that truth their own. They will need the help of the Holy Spirit. And sometimes he will use another human being as his "assistant" in the healing process. But healing can and will happen. The key is realizing that every human being bears this mark of heavenly excellence: Made in God's Image.

Of course, Scripture contains other reasons why we can feel good about ourselves. Jesus said we are to love others "as ourselves." The Christian in particular can rejoice that he or she is now an heir of the King of the universe. Finally, as we mentioned earlier, Jesus' death leaves no doubt as to how much he feels we're worth. According to 1 John 4:19, "We love because he first loved us." We can apply this passage not only to those around us, but also to ourselves!

Bridge

As we've seen, the Christian in particular has ample reason to harbor a sense of self-worth: We have been created in God's image. But we can help others feel good about themselves in a very practical way—by affirming one another. That's something we're going to do right now!

Activity: "Affirmation Diads"

Have the group divide into pairs. One person in each group is given a minute and a half to tell the listening partner of an achievement, talent, trait, or other source of personal pride. The partners then reverse roles, and another ninety seconds is given for the other person to talk. Finally, participants are asked to tell about their partners' accomplishments. A light-hearted addition (particularly in a small group format) is to applaud following each presentation.

"Affirmation Diads" is a simple, effective way to show affirmation for another while affording that individual the experience of being publicly praised.

Wrap-up

Several years ago, Yale University chemist Harold J. Morowitz set out to determine the dollar value of a human being. The various minerals and other elements found in the body were "priced out" at the current rates. When the numbers were finally totalled, the typical, healthy human body was found to be "worth" just over $6 million.[2]

But God's crowning result of creation—you and I—are price-*less* in his eyes. We are worth more than any amount of money, for the substance of our souls cannot be purchased. We are God's children, made in his image—reflections of the divine.[3]

Discussion Questions

1. Are there any Scriptural indications of self-esteem in the life of Jesus? (Give examples.)

2. Is the development of self-esteem primarily our responsibility or is it God's? Explain.
3. What are some specific things a person can do to develop self-esteem?
4. The apostle Paul speaks often of the need to deny "self." What does he mean?
5. Give at least five reasons why a healthy sense of self-esteem is important. (List on white board.)

Suggested Scripture

Genesis 1:26–27; Psalm 8:3–6; John 3:16; Romans 5:8; Ephesians 2:4–7.

For Further Reading

Bruce Narramore, *You're Someone Special* (Grand Rapids: Zondervan, 1978).

David A. Seamands, *Healing for Damaged Emotions* (Wheaton, Ill.: Victor Books, 1981).

Gary Smalley, *The Blessing* (Nashville: Thomas Nelson, 1986).

5

Sherlock Holmes and the Bible

Purpose

To demonstrate the need of considering context when interpreting Scripture.

Materials Needed

White board or newsprint, marker

Preparation

Cards for "Mixed Messages" activity

Introduction

For many individuals, reading the Bible is similar to spinning one's tires on ice—they just don't seem to get anywhere.

Although the reasons for this futility vary, there is one secret to studying the Bible which is often overlooked. It is a tool of biblical interpretation called contextualization. Simply stated, it means learning about the original circumstances surrounding a particular portion of Scripture. Who wrote it, why, and to whom it is directed are some of the important questions that context helps to answer. Understanding this concept can unlock the treasure chest of God's Word.

Illustration

The March 1950 *Reader's Digest* featured an article titled "The Case of the Baker Street Plans." The piece originally appeared in *The Baker Street Journal,* a magazine published by and for Sherlock Holmes buffs. The story which helps to illustrate the concept of contextualization begins with a brief explanation:

> In 1934 ten Sherlock Holmes addicts, headed by Christopher Morley, banded together as "The Baker Street Irregulars." Today the Irregulars have spread spontaneously all over the United States and abroad with branches named for various adventures of Holmes—for example, The Speckled Band of Boston, The Pondicherry Lodge of Springfield, Illinois, The Greek Interpreters of Pontiac, Michigan. The Five Orange Pips referred to below flourish in Westchester County, New York.[1]

The rest of the true story, written by Ellery Husted, goes like this:

> After waiting around Ford Island three weeks, my orders finally came: *Report Cincpac (Admiral Nimitz, Commander in Chief Pacific) Advanced Intelligence Headquarters, Guam. Passage via Air Transport. Proceed without delay.*
>
> An hour's paper work, 15 minutes' packing, and I made it a minute before the plane took off. There was a two-day hop ahead, and I'd forgotten to pack a book. On my way through the hangar I saw on a chair a paper-backed volume with no visible owner. The cover said: *Six Adventures of Sherlock Holmes.* I stole it without shame.
>
> After reading it twice, I wondered what I could do to make my monotonous trip less depressing. I pictured Sherlock Holmes and Dr. Watson seated comfortably before their fire at 221B Baker Street, and since I was an architect in peacetime it was natural to speculate as to what their rooms had looked like. Suddenly a thought burned through the cloud of my ennui. I retrieved the *Six Adventures* and prepared for another reading with re-awakened eyes. Scattered through each of the stories were disconnected

but explicit references to the physical arrangements of the famed rooms. I began to copy all references to them. When I had finished, and had sorted and assembled the architectural references, I found to my surprise that each fitted like a shaped piece into a picture puzzle. Then I reconstructed the plans and elevations of 221B. No line was drawn without confirmation from the text.

The complete work made a bulky package and on landing at Guam I was about to throw it away when I thought of my friend Dick Clarke, another Navy man and a member of The Five Orange Pips. It might amuse him to receive this bit of literary archaeology. I put the papers in an envelope addressed to Clarke, arranged for them to be sent by air mail, and forgot them in the more serious business of war.

Some months later the war ended and I got my orders home. I was cheerfully destroying officials papers when I was handed a large and familiar envelope covered with the ink of rubber stamps. It was my letter to Clarke come back to roost and I assumed that it had been sent off with too few stamps.

Next morning on the plane back to Pearl Harbor a blond young ensign in the seat ahead turned around and said, "Your name's Husted?"

I nodded.

"And how's Dr. Watson?" he asked with a grin.

I considered the question for a moment and realized the ensign must have been a Cincpac military censor. "I suppose you censored that Baker Street letter."

"Yeah. *And did it give us trouble.* They put the best brains in Guam on it, but nobody could make anything of it. It was obviously in code, but we couldn't break it, so we sent it to Pearl. They spent some time on it and sent it on to Washington, but it was no go. It came back to us, and we held it until the war was over."

I laughed and said, "You knew all about me. Why didn't you ask me about it?"

The ensign smiled. "Yeah, we knew all about you, but it wasn't that easy. We checked your handwriting with the letter and it didn't agree. Too jerky. And you'll agree that all that stuff about 221B Baker Street sounded queer. On any basis, the letter didn't make any sense."

I thought of the wavy handwriting caused by the undulations of air travel, of my mysterious disconnected passages lifted from the text, and especially of my enigmatic letter to Clarke:

Dear Dick: Tell your group of Peculiar Pips that 221B did exist, and that it has been resurrected by one who is not of you, but believes in you. I wish Holmes were with me to solve the riddle of the Empire. God bless you, and in the names of Holmes and Baker Street keep up the good fight.

Yours,
Husted

I could not but agree that the alerted censors had had cause for their suspicions, and was ruminating pleasantly over the extent of trouble I had probably caused when the blond head before me revolved again to say:

"And worst of all, my friend, Baker Street was the code name for [U.S. Office of Strategic Services] Headquarters, London."[2]

Bridge

Obviously confusion can result when a communique originally intended for one party is read by another. "The Case of the Baker Street Plans" has something to say to us concerning the way we interrupt another, *heavenly* communique—the Bible.

Activity: "Mixed Messages"

"Mixed Messages" is a fun activity that both enhances the preceding thoughts and leads into application of the concept of contextualization. The absurd results of the exercise will serve to impress more deeply the need for "rightly dividing the Word of truth."

Prior to the meeting, write each of the following Bible excerpts on individual cards, numbering them as indicated:

1. "I am the LORD . . . I will bring upon you sudden terror, wasting diseases and fever that will destroy your sight and drain away your life" (Lev. 26:1b, 16).

1A. "God is love" (1 John 4:16b).

2. "To the man who does not work but trusts God . . . his faith is credited as righteousness" (Rom. 4:5).

2A. ". . . a person is justified by what he does and not by faith alone . . ." (James 2:24).

3. "The LORD God said, 'It is not good for the man to be alone'" (Gen. 2:18).

3A. "It is good for a man not to marry" (1 Cor. 7:1b).

Distribute the cards at random, one card per person. Ask for card #1 to be read aloud, followed immediately by card #1A. Do the same with the other two sets of cards. The seeming contradiction of the corresponding cards will be readily apparent.

Bridge

There is no shortage of apparent biblical paradoxes. But rather than attempt to expose all these seeming contradictions in Scripture, let's try to understand them. One way to help do that is by viewing each passage in its original context. By looking at who the passage was first written to and under what circumstances, we can usually determine its original intent and better understand how it applies to us today. Let's try it!

Application

The first passage in the "Mixed Messages" exercise seems to paint a portrait of a God who enjoys distributing pain through terror, sickness, blindness, and death. But can this be the same God who is also defined as love personified? A look at the context of both passages clears up the problem.

The wrathful rendition of God's personhood is taken from the twenty-sixth chapter of Leviticus. The writer, who many believe to have been Moses, was recording God's setting forth to the Israelites both the punishment *and* rewards of serving him. The stiff-necked chosen people were in need of having a critical concept driven home—that it is only by serving Yahweh that their ultimate destiny will be fulfilled. Apparently the best way to communicate that truth was by showing the consequences of their decision: serve the Lord and they would get the Promised Land; discard the divine and they would die.

As for the more mellow passage, "God is love," it is found in the Book of First John, chapter four. Here the apostle is writing as a "spiritual father" to members of the body of Christ. Hence, he calls his readers "little children."

Besides being a general pastoral epistle, there was another purpose for this letter. Certain heresies had made their way into the church (see 1 John 2:18–19), and John was anxious that amidst the confusion the basics of the faith not be forgotten. Accordingly, one of the purposes of his little book was to help "foster the fundamentals," as it were. To achieve that end, John reduces the religious experience to its essence; centering much of his book around a three-word theme: "God is love."

Outside a logical frame of reference, the two passages seem to present God as being self-incongruent. But a look at the context of each helps clear up the problem.

The mystery of the second set of "Mixed Messages" can also be easily solved by viewing them in context. The Book of Romans, which is where Paul speaks of "trusting God" for one's righteousness, is primarily a letter of theology. James, however, is more concerned with "practical Christianity." Therefore, as commentator Burton Scott Easton says, he is writing to ". . . men and women desiring to fulfill properly the tasks of daily life." Easton concludes by saying, "Such teaching James gives them, that and no more."[3] While Paul wants no mistake made as to the source or root of salvation, James points out that works or "deeds" are the fruit of true conversion. By understanding the context, both views make sense.

The "Mixed Messages" having to do with marriage are also easier to understand when seen in their original settings. It is clear that marriage is a God-ordained institution, for it was the Almighty who said that it was "not good for the man to be alone." But a closer look at 1 Corinthians 7:1 shows that Paul was responding to a specific inquiry, for he begins his counsel by saying, "Now for the matters you wrote about" (1 Cor. 7:1a). He suggests that apparently for some, singleness was an acceptable status. But interestingly, immediately following is a section of practical advice written for husbands and wives. Clearly, marriage was also still a godly option!

Bridge

The problem areas of Scripture, such as apparent contradictions, can often be cleared up through contextualization. Bible dictionaries, commentaries, and other reference tools can help shed light on some of the puzzling areas. Reading a few verses that precede and follow that problem passage can also help.

But as Timothy wrote, "All Scripture is God-breathed" (2 Tim. 3:16). As such, it transcends human understanding.

It is true that many of the Bible's writings had a specific audience. But because Scripture is ultimately divinely inspired, there are also eternal principles that today's Christian is called to heed. Gleaning these nuggets of heavenly wisdom is the ultimate goal of Bible study.

Application

Here are a few suggestions for getting to the "principle of the thing."

First, having studied its original context, determine what need in today's world the counsel or topic discussed might address. Sometimes this will be obvious, but often a degree of contemplation and discussion with mature Christians is necessary.

Next, check these conclusions against other portions of Scripture on the same or a related topic. Are they congruent? Other proven works of faith such as classic Christian literature and reference tools may also shed light.

Finally, decide how this principle might be applied to an individual's life in practical terms. Then do it! Spiritual maturity is demonstrated by living out what you have learned.

Activity: "Principles in Practice"

Using the above concepts, solicit randomly from the group principles drawn either from the texts used in the "Mixed Messages" activity or some new ones. Here are a few possibilities: Deuteronomy 7:1–2; Matthew 5:38–42; 1 Corinthians 14:34–35; Galatians 3:28. Write them on a white board or newsprint, allowing for appropriate discussion. Ask for added scriptural support for the ideas set forth. Of course, it is possible that *no* principle is readily discernible. But encourage the group to consider why such a passage may have been included in the Bible. Finally, ask for a specific example of how each principle might be applied to a Christian's life.

Wrap-up

Deciphering the Bible can be a challenge. While many things can help solve its mysteries, looking at the context of a passage is a good place to start. But beyond all methods of human deduction lies the greatest resource of all—the help of the Holy Spirit. Through prayer ask God to assist in the process of understanding his Word. As Sherlock Holmes would have said, "It's elementary."

Discussion Questions

1. Is interpreting the Bible ultimately a subjective or an objective matter? Explain.
2. Besides context, what are some other important things to consider when interpreting Scripture?
3. The Bible contains passages that are particularly difficult to interpret. What are some reasons for this?
4. Certain denominations lift Bible verses from their context to lend support to their doctrines. Can you give any examples of this? (See *Scripture Twisting*, pp. 80–82.)
5. Some individuals believe God communicated to the Bible writers exactly what to write. Is this a sound theory of inspiration? What are some others?

Suggested Scripture

Psalm 119:105; 2 Timothy 2:15, 3:15–17; 2 Peter 3:15–16.

For Further Reading

Max Anders, *Thirty Days to Understanding Your Bible* (Brentwood, Tenn.: Wolgemuth & Hyatt, 1988).

James W. Sire, *Scripture Twisting* (Downers Grove, Ill.: InterVarsity, 1980).

6

Friendly Advice

Purpose

To affirm the need for meaningful Christian relationships, and explore the dynamics involved in establishing and maintaining them.

Materials Needed

White board or newsprint, marker

Preparation

Photocopy four "Dave's Date with Danger" scripts, found in Appendix. Assign the various parts prior to the meeting. The drama will be presented in "readers' theater" style.

Introduction

Eventually, nearly everyone needs a friend. But establishing a meaningful friendship is sometimes difficult. Today's busy world often leaves little time for sharing our hurts and hopes with another. Nevertheless, the need for intimacy at varying levels still exists.

An episode of the television series *I Love Lucy* portrayed just how desperate one can be for friendship. Lucy Ricardo, played by actress Lucille Ball, was convinced that she had virtually no meaningful relationships. Desperate, Lucy formed a Salvation Army-like band of loners—"Friends of the Friendless"—to broadcast the news of their pitiful situation. The results, however, were far different from the impression Lucy had planned. Instead of being dramatic, the incident was hilarious. But hidden between the humorous lines there is a serious truth—everybody needs a friend: someone with whom to share laughter and love, triumph and tragedy.

Bridge

For many, childhood conjures up thoughts of friendship. The reasons for this may vary. Perhaps there was more to share, maybe less to hide. Whatever the reasons, looking to the past can help us recapture some important elements of friendship.

Activity: "Cherished Friends of Childhood"

Have each person in the group share a childhood experience of friendship (positive or negative). Encourage participants to include names, places, etc., whenever possible and appropriate. This will reveal intriguing and meaningful aspects of group members' past experience while focusing on friendship.

Bridge

Sharing memories of childhood relationships is a valuable experience. Too often the feelings surrounding our earlier experiences are forgotten. But there is one thing that looking to the past cannot do—satisfy a longing in the *present* for meaningful friendship.

Although some individuals have opted for a solitary life, human beings were designed as social creatures. As Jerry and Mary White have written in their book, *Friends and Friendship*, ". . . no one can have a meaningful existence without love and friendship. They are the substance of our emotional life."[1]

Yet loneliness continues to thrive. If friendship is in such high demand, why are so many lives lived out alone?

One possible answer is that many individuals simply do not know how to find a friend. These same persons may suffer from the delusion that quality relationships just evolve—that "chemistry" is the ultimate criteria. But the science of friendship goes much deeper!

While the Bible is first a revelation of how God relates to his children, it also contains helpful insight concerning human relationships. Perhaps no finer example of friendship exists than the story of David and Jonathan. A closer look at their relationship will help reveal some of the secrets of lasting friendship.

Activity: "Dave's Date with Danger"

Use the script beginning on page 58 to tell the story of David and Jonathan's friendship.

Have the previously selected participants (those who have been assigned parts and received scripts[2]) come forward and present "Dave's Date with Danger" in readers' theater style. Readers' theater is simply a group dramatic reading. The script is taken from the twentieth chapter of First Samuel (NEB). Encourage the readers (this includes the narrator, who fills in between the dialog) to use the appropriate inflections. Physical actions are unnecessary, although an uninhibited cast might find this a colorful addition.

Ask the audience to note specific characteristics of David and Jonathan's friendship which surface during the narrative. These notes will be used immediately following the presentation.

Bridge

Many important elements of lasting friendship are found throughout the story of David and Jonathan. A look at some of the traits of their friendship can help us strengthen our own relationships.

Interaction

Following the presentation of "Dave's Date with Danger," randomly solicit from the audience different attributes of friendship gleaned from the story. Write these qualities in a column on the white board or newsprint, labeling it *Attributes*. Next, ask group members to submit words which describe traits opposite of those just mentioned. Write these in a column which corresponds to the previous one, calling this list *Obstacles* (to friendship). Finally, have the audience supply traits for both columns based on their personal observations of friendship—factors which may not have been apparent in this particular narrative. Use the following starters as necessary to facilitate the activity:

Attributes	*Obstacles*
Loyalty	Disloyalty
Transparency	Concealment
Devotion	Apathy
Willingness to defend	Passivity
Intimacy	Aloofness
Trustworthiness	Undependability
Other-centeredness	Self-centeredness
Listening skills	Disinterest/disattachment
Affirmation	Belittlement/discounting

Personal Observations
Willingness to rebuke (when appropriate)
Zealous, not jealous in friendship

Conclude the experiment by suggesting that when it comes to friendship, the first column (along with the personal observation attributes) contains qualities to be cultivated, while the latter column depicts traits to be eradicated.

Application

Nurturing positive traits of friendship can help us establish rich relationships. But along with such specific qualities, there are also some broad principles of friendship which, when heeded, can facilitate the process of finding and keeping good friends:

1. Know what kind of friend you need. Are you looking for a fellow pool shark or a prayer partner? Do you need someone to disciple you? Perhaps you're hoping to form a new friendship based on what you can offer the other person—an excellent approach. Whatever the case, deciding on the goal of a desired relationship will help give you focus in your pursuit of friends. Of course, just because someone might not feel compelled to spend time with you in one area doesn't mean you can't have a close friendship in another. Be open to all possibilities. Friendship is a valuable commodity.

2. Pace your companionship. Moving in too quickly is often responsible for quenching what might have otherwise become a meaningful friendship. The roots of comradery must take hold before the fruit of friendship can be picked. Give the plant time to grow.

3. Act on your friendly intentions. Wishing will never net a friendship—you've got to go out fishing. Avoid the stress of wondering if the other person will take the first step—take it yourself. You have nothing to lose except your loneliness.

4. Process rejection appropriately. Not every attempt at friendship is destined to succeed. Understand that, and realize that rejection is more often the result of poor dynamics than a personal affront. Let this one go, but don't kick your self-concept around the block and withdraw. Instead, learn what didn't work and apply the knowledge as you reach out again. Someone needs you.

5. Pursue "faith-filled" friendships first. It is said that Jesus was a "friend of sinners." But it is significant that he chose to share himself in a deeper way with a select few—specifically the twelve disciples and certain other God-fearing individuals. In the tradition of Jesus, today's Christian is called to minister to people across life's spectrum. But it is appropriate that the circle of friendship begin with fellow believers. Branch out from there, always keeping the true Vine as your common ground.

Wrap-up

Friends. They are a God-sent sweetener of life. Theirs is a richness, however, of which too few partake. But those who have savored the flavor of a special friendship know that here is a delicacy which they can not do without. Perhaps the time has come for you to experience this delectable fruit called friendship.

"DAVE'S DATE WITH DANGER" SCRIPT[3]

Characters: David
              Jonathan
              Saul
              Narrator

Production Notes: "Dave's Date with Danger" is designed to be presented in "readers' theater" style. Readers should stand facing the audience; a semicircle works well. Use dramatic inflections and actions as appropriate.

Narrator: Few things in life threaten some individuals more than a loss of power. Such was the possibility King Saul was facing. In an effort to retain the throne of Israel, he decided to put to death his potential successor, David, the son of Jesse. The Bible relates one attempt by Saul to end David's life. Ironically, it is Saul's own son Jonathan who helps David avoid an untimely death. The story of this incredible friendship is found in 1 Samuel 20, where David is desperately seeking an answer from his trusted friend, Jonathan:

David: *(Pleading.)* What have I done? What is my offense? What does your father think I have done wrong, that he seeks my life?

Jonathan: God forbid! There is no thought of putting you to death. I am sure my father will not do anything whatever without telling me. Why should my father hide such a thing from me? I cannot believe it!

David: I am ready to swear to it: your father has said to himself, "Jonathan must not know this or he will resent it," because he knows that you have a high regard for me. As the LORD lives, your life upon it, there is only a step between me and death.

Jonathan: What do you want me to do for you?

David: *(Thoughtfully.)* It is new moon tomorrow, and I ought to dine with the king. Let me go and lie hidden in the fields until the third evening. If your father happens to miss me, then say, "David asked me for leave to pay a rapid visit to his home in Bethlehem, for it is the annual sacrifice there for the whole family." If he says, "Well and good," that will be a good sign for me; but if he flies into a rage, you will know that he is set on doing me wrong. *(Seriously.)* My lord, keep faith with me; for you and I have entered into a solemn agreement before the LORD. Kill me yourself if I am guilty. Why let me fall into your father's hands?

Jonathan: *(Astonished.)* God forbid! If I find my father set on doing you wrong I will tell you.

David: How will you let me know if he answers harshly?

Jonathan: *(Pause.)* Come with me into the fields.

Narrator: So they went together into the fields, and Jonathan said to David,

Jonathan: *(Intensely.)* I promise you, David, in the sight of the LORD the God of Israel, this time tomorrow I will sound my father for the third time and, if he is well disposed to you, I will send and let you know. If my father means mischief, the LORD do the same to me and more, if I do not let you know and get you safely away. The LORD be with you as he has been with my father! I know that as long as I live you will show me faithful friendship, as the LORD requires; and if I should die, you will continue loyal to my family forever. When the LORD rids the earth of all David's enemies, may the LORD call him to account if he and his house are no longer my friends.

Narrator: Jonathan pledged himself afresh to David because of his love for him, for he loved him as himself. Then he said to him,

Jonathan: Tomorrow is the new moon, and you will be missed when your place is empty. So go down at nightfall for the third time to the place where you hid on the evening of the feast and stay by the mound there. Then I will shoot three arrows towards it, as though I were aiming at a mark. Then I will send my boy to find the arrows. If I say to him, "Look, the arrows are on this side of you, pick them up," then you can come out of hiding. You will be quite safe, I swear it; for there will be nothing amiss. But if I say to the lad, "Look, the arrows are on the other side of you, further on," then the LORD has said that you must go; the LORD stand witness between us for ever to the pledges we have exchanged.

Narrator: So David hid in the fields. The new moon came, the dinner was prepared, and the king sat down to eat. Saul took his customary seat by the wall, and Abner sat beside him; Jonathan too was present *(slight pause)*, but David's place was empty. That day Saul said nothing, for he thought that David was absent by some chance, perhaps because he was ritually unclean. But on the second day, the day after the new moon, David's place was still empty, and Saul said to his son Jonathan, "Why has not the son of Jesse come to the feast, either yesterday or today?"

Jonathan: David asked permission to go to Bethlehem. He asked my leave and said, "Our family is holding a sacrifice in the town and my brother himself has ordered me to be there. Now, if you have any regard for me, let me slip away to see my brothers." That is why he has not come to dine with the king.

Saul: *(Angrily.)* You son of a crooked and unfaithful mother! You have made friends with the son of Jesse only to bring shame on yourself and dishonour on your mother; I see how it will be. As long as Jesse's son remains alive on earth, neither you nor your crown will be safe. Send at once and fetch him; he deserves to die.

Jonathan: *(Outraged.)* He deserves to die! Why? What has he done?

Narrator: At that, Saul picked up his spear and threatened to kill him; and he knew that his father was bent on David's death. Jonathan left the table in a rage and ate nothing on the second day of the festival; for he was indignant on David's behalf because his father had humiliated him.

Next morning, Jonathan went out into the fields to meet David at the appointed time, taking a young boy with him. He said to the boy,

Jonathan: Run and find the arrows; I am going to shoot.

Narrator: The boy ran on, and he shot the arrows over his head. When the boy reached the place where Jonathan's arrows had fallen, Jonathan called out after him,

Jonathan: Look, the arrows are beyond you. Hurry! No time to lose! Make haste!

Narrator: The boy gathered up the arrows and brought them to his master; but only Jonathan and David knew what this meant; the boy knew nothing. Jonathan handed his weapons to the boy and told him to take them back to the city. When the boy had gone, David got up from behind the mound and bowed humbly three times. Then they kissed one another and shed tears together, until David's grief was even greater than Jonathan's. Jonathan said to David,

Jonathan: Go in safety; we have pledged each other in the name of the LORD who is witness for ever between you and me and between your descendants and mine.

Narrator: David went off at once, while Jonathan returned to the city. Their ways had for now parted, but through friendship they were forever united.

Discussion Questions

1. Some would suggest that males have a more difficult time than females when it comes to sharing intimately with each other on a friendship basis. Do you agree or disagree? If agreed, what might be the reason/s for this difficulty?
2. What are some reasons why certain individuals seem to have an easier time making friends than others?
3. Several years ago there was a popular tune titled, "Everybody Needs Somebody Sometime." Is this true? Can you think of someone who has boasted of being self-fulfilled without friends? To the best of your knowledge, did his or her experience bear out their claim?
4. Is a Christian ever allowed to terminate a friendship? If so, suggest some circumstances that might allow for this.

5. Do you agree or disagree with the idea that the Christian's most intimate friends should be fellow believers? Why/why not?

Suggested Scripture

Exodus 33:7–11; Proverbs 17:17, 18:24; John 15:13.

For Further Reading

Alan Loy McGinniss, *The Friendship Factor* (Minneapolis: Augsburg, 1979).

Jerry and Mary White, *Friends and Friendship: The Secrets of Drawing Closer* (Colorado Springs: NavPress, 1982).

7

A Strong Case for Weakness

Purpose

To show how God's sovereignty and creative power brings dignity and purpose to human weakness.

Materials Needed

Pencils, index cards

Preparation

Prepare all cards as indicated in the activity "Healer's Helper Classified Ads."

Introduction

At first glance, some things just don't seem to belong together. But a second look often proves otherwise. Take for example Milton Hershey's creative candy, "bittersweet chocolate." If the stuff is bitter, how can it be sweet? Conversely, if the stuff is sweet, how can it be bitter? Who knows? But it is.

Candy companies are not the only people who have fused seeming opposites. Etymologists have placed words together that shouldn't be, calling the hybrid phrases *oxymorons*. "Reginald was sadly amused" is a good example of an oxymoron. Even the prolific writer James Thurber employed the oxymoronic device. His word picture, "a little bit big," seems terribly incongruous. Apparently, however, in the world of oxymorons, all things are possible.

The examples of such self-contradicting combinations could go on. Not that all things that go together but shouldn't are opposites. We may each have our own combination which has worked, but shouldn't have!

Activity: "Oppalikes"

This activity, in a relaxed and potentially humorous way, shows the strange combinations in life which somehow end up "working" for the individual/s involved.

Ask group members to think of an apparently ominous combination in their experience which had a successful outcome. This could be something as simple as a peanut butter and banana sandwich, or as significant as an interracial marriage. Allow a brief time for thinking (background music may be appropriate during this time), then have the participants tell their recollections.

Bridge

As we have seen, opposites, or at least apparent incongruencies, can often work together. But perhaps nowhere is this truth more evident than in Second Corinthians 12:10. Let's look at the apostle Paul's "weak strongman"!

Biblical Perspective

The chapter begins with Paul's telling of his knowing a man who had been to the *third heaven*. Scholars are uncertain what this *third heaven* actually was. Paul, however, felt privileged to have made this man's acquaintance. But it seems that something was allowed to come his way to help keep Paul humble. Beginning with verse seven of Second Corinthians 12 we read:

To keep me from becoming conceited because of these surpass-ingly great revelations, there was given me a thorn in my flesh, a messenger of Satan, to torment me. Three times I pleaded with the Lord to take it away from me. But he said to me, "My grace is sufficient for you, for my power is made perfect in weakness."

Paul is convinced, indeed convicted that, with Christ in control, his struggles can make him stronger. His concluding thoughts on the subject are found beginning with verse nine: "Therefore, I will boast all the more gladly about my weaknesses, so that Christ's power may rest on me. That is why, for Christ's sake, I delight in weaknesses, in insults, in hardships, in persecutions, in difficulties." Paul then ends with a paradox par excellence: "For when I am weak, then I am strong."

As Paul's list suggests, "thorns" come in many forms. And while times may have changed, strife is still with us. Weaknesses? Even the strongest human has them. As for insults, no one's skin is thick enough not to have felt their occasional sting. Hardships? The local social services agencies can furnish an ample listing of those in need. Nor are persecutions a thing of the past. And difficulties? Joni Eareckson-Tada, a quadriplegic herself, in her book *Choices, Changes,* shares a small sampling of such despair. She has returned to Los Rancho Hospital in Southern California, where she had years earlier undergone physical therapy. Joni has been conversing with an employee:

"You met the guys in O.T.?" [Debbie] asks, turning the conversation away from herself.

""Yes." I nod and then add, "Things in occupational therapy haven't changed much . . . potholders and paints and stuff. But those guys seem to have a good attitude about it."

Debbie's smile fades. "Well, not all of them. Did you meet the boy with the halo cast?"

I nod again.

"His parents don't want anything to do with him. He broke his neck in a motorcycle accident, driving when he was drunk. They figure he got himself into this mess, he can get himself out." She sighs and shakes her head.

I wince and look toward the window of the therapy room. I wish I had said more to him.

"And the good-looking paraplegic? His wife just filed for divorce. I've tried talking to him about God, but he just won't listen. He's losing himself . . . in pity. In drugs."

I stare at the therapy room windows. The stories she relates are strikingly similar to many I heard when I was at Rancho as a patient years ago. But they didn't touch me then as they do now.[1]

Thorns. None will escape their pointed pain. But as Joni Eareckson-Tada learned, thorns can either break you down or make you stronger. The secret lies in giving them over to God. By so doing, as Paul discovered, the weight of dependency shifts from self to Christ. That is the formula for growing in grace.

But there is another positive aspect of being weak in ourselves, yet strong through Christ. While you may have a personal desire to be healed of a difficulty, or thorn, God may have a grander purpose in mind for your pain. When human thorns are given over to his power, their owners are enabled to become "Healer's Helpers," persons well-qualified to assist the Holy Spirit in the "healing" of another. Put another way, misery is often the 'boot camp' of ministry. No one can comfort a hurting person better than one who has personally been there. Let's explore just how that can happen.

Activity: "Healer's Helper Classified Ads"

This activity is designed to show how human weaknesses, or "thorns," when given over to God's power and creativity can become tools for ministry.

Divide the audience into four groups. Distribute one 3" X 5" index card with the heading "Healing Wanted" to each group. Or print these four situations in 3" X 5" boxes to be photocopied and cut. In addition, one of the following situations should appear on each card:

1. I am a nineteen-year-old student attending a state university. Last year I was a consistent weekend party person. This was a great way to make friends, but a lousy way to live. I

made a commitment during the summer to maintain the relationships but quit doing the stupid things I was doing to myself. Little by little, though, my former "friends" are leaving me out of their lives. I really need someone to talk to. Can you help?

2. I am a forty-five-year-old male and a Vietnam veteran. I have a purple heart and a wheelchair to prove it. When I returned from Nam, my wife seemed willing to accept the paralysis. But something, or more accurately someone, has changed her mind. She left this morning. I don't know whether it's worth trying to go on. I am desperate for some answers.

3. I am a twenty-nine-year-old street person. I have tried many times to kick my booze habit and get on the road to a better life. But sometimes I feel like I'm destined to die in the gutter. Nobody wants to give guys like me a break—at least not doing something that's legal. Does anybody out there care?

4. I am a single thirty-three-year-old entrepreneur. One year ago I left a position with Tech-Systems to start my own business. Unfortunately, my dream is not being realized, and the business is failing. I see filing for bankruptcy as my only option. I have always been plagued by low self-esteem and had hoped that a successful business venture would help. Obviously, the current situation is causing the opposite to occur. I need someone to turn to. If you are qualified to help, please reply soon!

Each "ad" is to be responded to (by the small group) by supplying a one-or two-paragraph hypothetical, yet realistic, "application for 'employment'." But the position of "Healer's Helper" is to be gained based on *"redeemed" weakness,* or "thorns," which have been committed to Christ, not human skills or strengths. An example response to number four above might be:

Name: Barbara Hansen
Age: 66

Situation Summary: Barbara was recently forced to retire from her position as administrator with the local Small Business Administration office.

Qualifications for being a Healer's Helper to this individual: As a result of my termination, I have had to overcome the loss and ensuing bitterness it brought. Sharing the details of this process with someone in your circumstances could prove helpful to you at this time. In addition, since I now find myself with more free time than in the past, I would be willing to devote some of it to consulting with you regarding alternatives for the future of your business venture.

Allow the groups 5–7 minutes to prepare their responses. Encourage the participants to avoid, if possible, simply responding as one whose situation has been identical to the advertiser's. Instead, suggest that replies be based on appropriate *principles* of healing drawn from the respondent's hypothetical situation. At the end of the time allowed, have each group tell both their situation and the group's collective response/resume.

The idea behind this exercise is to portray more than a *silver-lining* approach to problems. It is to help individuals begin to see how God can use one's hurts in the healing process of another. Deepen this concept by pointing out that, while human creativity can discover potential strength in weakness, how much more can God, "who is able to do immeasurably more than all we ask" (Eph. 3:20), provide opportunities for turning struggles into strengths.

Wrap-up

Thorns can either destroy us or they can drive us to depend more on God, to be used of him. From Joseph to Job to the apostle Paul, the Bible tells us that there is purpose in our pain. The weak-strongman is no absurdity. It is simply another of God's "impossible possibilities." Our weaknesses do become our strengths when our "thorns" are taken to the throne of God.

Discussion Questions

1. Besides those already mentioned, what are some biblical examples of individuals using their weakness to glorify God?
2. What are some effective ways to help an apathetic individual become motivated to turn a weakness into a strength?
3. What are some guidelines to follow in deciding if and when others should be told about a former weakness?
4. Does the experience of having been through a time of difficulty automatically qualify one to be a "Healer's Helper"? Why/why not? If not, what further requirements might be necessary?
5. Who are some "Healer's Helpers" who have made a significant impact upon your own life?

Suggested Scripture

The Book of Job; Romans 8:17; 2 Corinthians 1:3–7, 12:1–10; Philippians 3:7–11; Hebrews 4:15.

For Further Reading

Joni Eareckson-Tada, *Choices, Changes* (Grand Rapids: Zondervan, 1986).

Tim Hansel, *You Gotta Keep Dancin'* (Elgin, Ill.: David C. Cook Publishing Company, 1985).

David Seamands, *Healing Grace* (Wheaton, Ill.: Victor, 1988).

Philip Yancey, *Where Is God When It Hurts?* (Grand Rapids: Zondervan, 1977).

8

Risky Business

Purpose

To show that intelligent, *redemptive* risk adds dimension to life and provides unique opportunities for Christian service and personal growth.

Materials Needed

White board or newsprint, marker

Preparation

The initials from each name listed in the activity "Chance of a Lifetime" should be written in column form on the white board or newsprint.

Optional Warm-up Activity: "Reflecting on Risk"

At random, ask individuals to tell about one of the following situations: (1) A risk which he/she has gladly taken, (2) A risk taken which he/she regrets, or (3) A risk which he/she would like to take.

Introduction

In his book, *Who Switched the Price Tags?*, Tony Campolo documents the results of an intriguing sociological study. Each of the fifty participants was over the age of ninety-five and had been asked to respond to one question: "If you could live your life over again, what would you do differently?" One of the things consistently reported by many of these old folks was this: If they could do it differently, *they would take more risks.*[1]

This is worth pondering. What is risk? One dictionary defines it as "a chance of encountering harm or loss; hazard; danger." If true, such a description gives reason to question why the surveyed senior citizens wished that they had done it more often!

Obviously, not all risks are a sure thing. If they were, more would undoubtedly be taken. But while the majority chose security, there have been those who have taken their chances and—for better or worse—reaped the rewards of their risk. Let's consider a few of these people.

Activity: "Chance of a Lifetime"

This activity is a form of "word association." Call out each name listed below to a different individual in the audience. Point out that each is known to have taken a risk in life. Immediately after hearing the name, the person called is to say aloud the first adjective (a word of description) that he or she associates with that name. The leader (or assistant) then writes that word following the appropriate initials on the board or newsprint (as described in Preparation). Do this for each of the following names:

1. Joan of Arc	9. Rahab
2. Christopher Columbus	10. Rock Hudson
3. John De Lorean	11. Amelia Earhart
4. Donald Trump	12. Martin Luther King, Jr.
5. Christa McAuliffe	13. Evil Knievel
6. Oliver North	14. Jesse James
7. Gary Hart	15. Elijah
8. Mother Teresa	

(If desired, add names from current events.)

After all of the words have been recorded, point out the varying responses. While each individual named had taken a risk in life, the words used to describe the person suggests an impression their particular risk has made on another (in this case the person responding).

"Chance of a Lifetime" is designed to show that *every* risk produced consequences, good or bad.

Bridge

Intrinsically risk is neither good nor bad. But as the previous experience has shown, risk reaps results. For better or worse, risk changes lives.

It is true that results *can* sometimes serve as an indicator of a risk's worthiness. But is the end product an accurate barometer of the merit of a given risk? If not, what criteria may be used in deciding whether taking a chance in a given situation is wise? Let's look at a true story which will allow us to grapple with those questions.

Case Study: "Operation Auca"

On January 3, 1956, five men took a risk for God. Feeling led by him, this quintet of dedicated missionaries had decided to attempt to establish contact with Ecuador's Auca Indians. They were aware that the term *Auca* meant "savage" in the local dialect. They also knew that the title was well-deserved. In 1942, three employees of the Shell Oil Company were killed while prospecting for oil in Auca territory. The following year the number rose to eight. And these were not the first of the Indians' victims. Of the apparent randomness of the Auca slayings, Elisabeth Elliot, wife of one of the five missionaries wrote: "One fact only seems firmly established: the white man is unwanted. When he sets foot within the area that the Aucas have marked off for themselves, *he risks his life,*" (italics supplied).[2]

Nevertheless, the five men had purposed to serve the Lord among the various Indian tribes of Ecuador. Their respective decisions had not been made lightly.

During college Jim Elliot had spent much of a ten-day period in prayer. The issue: whether or not to enter fulltime mission service. The answer seemed to be an unequivocal "yes."

Pete Fleming was a longtime friend of Elliot's. After grappling with God during his graduate studies, Fleming decided to serve the One whom he had questioned. He wrote his fiancee, "I think a 'call' to the mission field is no different than any other means of guidance . . . A call is nothing more or less than obedience to the will of God. . . ."

Another friend of Jim Elliot's, Ed McCully, was a law student at Marquette University. He had taken a night job as a hotel clerk and would often read his Bible during free moments. Convicted by a passage in Nehemiah, he wrote a letter to Jim Elliot. Part of it read: "I have one desire now—to live a life of reckless abandon for the Lord, putting all my energy and strength into it. Maybe he'll send me someplace where the name of Jesus Christ is unknown." Ed and his wife Marilou would one day sense that call.

Nate Saint and his wife Marj had come to Ecuadorian Indian territory in 1948. Theirs was an aviation ministry in conjunction with the Missionary Aviation Fellowship. Medicine and other items were gotten more readily thanks to Nate's little Piper.

In 1953, Roger and Barbara Youderian, along with their six-month-old daughter Beth Elaine came to assume duties at the Macuma mission station in Ecuador. Earlier, in a letter to his mother, Roger had written: "Ever since I accepted Christ as my personal Saviour last fall . . . I've felt the call to either missionary, social or ministerial work . . . Can't say now what the calling will be but I want to be a witness for Him and live following Him every second of my life." To Roger Youderian, the call to the mission field was confirmed in his soul.

By 1954, both of the bachelors, Jim Elliot and Pete Fleming, had married. All five of the missionary families had now come into contact with each other. One goal was shared by all: to reach out with the gospel to the killer Auca Indians.

There were, however, moments of reticence. Pete wrote, "The thought scares me at times but I am ready. We have believed God for miracles, and this may include the Aucas. It has got to be by miracles in response to faith. No lesser expedient is a shortcut. O God, guide us!"

On September 19, 1955, Nate Saint and Ed McCully spotted an Auca settlement from the air. It was to be dubbed "Terminal City."

Months of collective brainstorming and preparation followed that initial sighting. In a gesture of friendliness, gifts and photographs of themselves were dropped from the air. The Aucas responded, eventually tying a return gift on the line dangling from the plane. Ed McCully's diary records the event: "Nate made a perfect drop. I held the line and could feel their holding onto it. They cut the pot off—and tied something on! When we got back to Arajuno we found that it was a *llaitu* or headband of woven feathers. A real answer to prayer; another sign to proceed . . ."

After several such signs throughout the next few weeks, the date was set: January 3, 1956 the plane would set down at Palm Beach, a clearing in Auca territory.

That Tuesday, after landing, a camp-like setting began taking shape. Here the men would anxiously await the arrival of the Aucas, for to venture unbidden into their village was not an option.

By Thursday evening there had been no contact made by the Indians. But Nate Saint wrote that evening, "We find that we have friendlier feeling for these fellows all the time." He then went on: "We must not let that lead us to carelessness."

Friday morning, 11:15. Apparently in response to Ed's calling into the jungle, three Auca Indians stepped into the open across the river. There was one man accompanied by two women. They gestured for someone to come over to their side of the river. Jim Elliot cautiously entered the water. The Indians followed and Jim led them back to his own side of the river. By referring to their phrase books, the missionaries were able to convey the idea to the trio that they need not be afraid. The man, whom the five arbitrarily called "George," took an interest in the plane. Nate took him up, flying over the Auca village still several miles away. It would be the first of three rides for the native.

That afternoon the trio departed, leaving the five missionaries to rejoice. Eventually, Nate and Pete returned to the mission station, while Jim, Ed, and Roger sat out an uneventful Saturday.

Sunday morning, as Nate and Pete climbed into the plane to return to Palm Beach, Pete called out: "So long, girls. Pray. I believe today's the day."

At twelve-thirty Nate radioed back to base that a "commission of ten" Aucas had been seen making their way toward the camp from Terminal City. "Looks like they'll be here for the early afternoon service. Pray for us. This *is* the day! Will contact you next at four-thirty."

At four-thirty the airways were silent. Throughout the night the radio was monitored, but there was no word from the men.

By seven o'clock Monday morning, January 9, a colleague of Nate Saint's, Johnny Keenan, was in the air flying toward Palm Beach. By nine-thirty the first report came to Marj Saint. She relayed this message to the other wives: "Johnny has found the plane on the beach. All of the fabric is stripped off. There is no sign of the fellows."

The search continued until on Wednesday, January 11, Johnny Keenan spotted a body floating facedown in the river. A closer look revealed a broken lance protruding from the hip. Around it was wrapped a gospel tract.

By Wednesday afternoon the United States Air Force had joined in the search. It was again Johnny Keenan, however, who spotted the second body.

On Thursday two canoes of Indians from another tribe were encountered. One of the Indians who had been converted to Christ by Ed McCully informed the search party that they had found Ed's body on the beach. It was never recovered by the searchers.

By Friday, January 13, 1956, the two remaining bodies had been found. The search was over. Five missionaries, certain of their calling to minister among the Auca Indians, had been killed by the ones they longed to serve.[3]

Discussion

Stimulate discussion on wisdom in risk-taking by immediately asking the question, "Was Operation Auca a 'good' risk?" Allow ample time for various responses. While maintaining focus of the issues is necessary during the discussion time, do not force a preconceived opinion. If possible, direct the discussion so that participants consider the dynamics involved in the decision-making process of the five missionaries. This will help foster a productive learning experience, rather than merely casting judgment on the martyrs.

Bridge

Apparently Nate Saint foresaw the potential for controversy in Operation Auca. Less than a month before his death he wrote, "As we weigh the future and seek the will of God, does it seem right that we should hazard our lives for just a few savages?" He answered affirmatively, reasoning that "it is the simple intimation of the prophetic Word that there shall be some from every tribe in His presence in the last day and in our hearts we feel that it is pleasing to Him that we should interest ourselves in making an opening into the Aucas' prison for Christ."[4]

The value of Operation Auca may never be agreed on this side of heaven. But one thing seems clear: a story of risking one's life for the sake of another's redemption is a tale worth being told.

Biblical Perspective

The Bible shows us some key ingredients in "good" risk-taking. A look at a few of the biggest risk-takers of Scripture—Abraham, David, Elijah, and others—reveals at least two common factors. First, they had a solid relationship with God. And second, their risks were redemptive at their core. Their "gambles" were taken with God's purposes in mind, the results designed to benefit something or someone other than themselves.

Few, if any, theories are foolproof. But the theory of redemptive risk works well in many instances.

Are you afraid to risk loving again? Redemptive risk says look outside yourself and realize that someone else may need your love.

Should you take a chance on the stock market? Redemptive risk says "Ultimately, when and where can my money best be used for others?" It may be that such a choice would be your best bet. But it could also be that a starving child will survive another day because you gave today.

Whatever the risk you are facing, Scripture has made clear that a redemptive risk, taken in relationship to God, often reaps positive results.

As Abraham left Ur of the Chaldees, as Elijah called down fire from heaven, and as David took on the giant Goliath, each knew that the risk he was taking was designed to reflect the glory of God. Perhaps the risk taken by five missionaries in Ecuador was also made with the same thought in mind. They knew in whom they had believed, and to further his cause was, for them, worth the risk.

Application

Obviously, there is a limit to the energy one can devote to a decision involving risk. But there are some specific actions which one can take to help avoid unnecessary agony when facing risk:

1. Ask yourself, "Will taking this risk afford me the opportunity to better love God, myself, and others?"
2. Count the cost(s), to yourself and others, of a given risk, and weigh them against the potential rewards.
3. Pray that your choices and timing will reflect God's sovereign will.
4. When the results of a well-reasoned risk prove negative, reflect, do not ruminate. Negative thinking will not bring about a positive result.
5. With God as your guide, risk again. When we pursue only that which is certain, we run a still-greater risk: a life of mediocrity. Someone has put it this way:

Risks

To laugh is to risk appearing the fool.
To weep is to risk appearing sentimental.
To reach out for another is to risk involvement.
To expose feelings is to risk exposing your true self.
To place your ideas, your dreams before a crowd is to risk their loss.
To love is to risk not being loved in return.

To live is to risk dying.
To hope is to risk despair.
To try is to risk failure.
But risks must be taken because the greatest hazard in life is to risk nothing.
The person who risks nothing does nothing, has nothing, and is nothing.
They may avoid suffering and sorrow but they cannot learn, feel, change, grow, or live.
Chained by their certitudes they are a slave; they have forfeited their freedom.
Only a person who risks is free.

—Anonymous

Wrap-up

Jesus Christ himself took the biggest redemptive risk of all time, for he had the most to lose—a world dying to sin. Like so many Christians since, the urge to share the good news about God drove him to take the risk of being rejected. And while he was indeed destined to love something—his very life—the story would not end there. For he would rise again and enjoy the reward of his risk throughout eternity.

Discussion Questions

1. Define "good" risk and "bad" risk.
2. What advantage, if any, does the Christian have in assuming risk?
3. Should Christians always avoid unnecessary risk? Why/why not?
4. What are some biblical examples of taking risks? Was the outcome positive or negative? Why?
5. Peter Drucker has suggested that there are four types of risks: (1) the risk one must accept, (2) the risk one can afford to take, (3) the risk which one cannot afford to take, and (4) the risk which one cannot afford not to take. Is this assessment of risk correct? What might be an example of each?

Suggested Scripture

1 Samuel 17; 1 Kings 18:1–39; Matthew 21:12–13; Philippians 2:25–30.

For Further Reading

Anthony Campolo, *Who Switched the Price Tags?* (Waco, Tex.: Word, 1987).

Elisabeth Elliot (editor), *The Journals of Jim Elliot* (Old Tappan, NJ: Fleming H. Revell, 1978).

Elisabeth Elliot, *Through Gates of Splendor* (New York: Harper, 1957).

John Urquhart and Klaus Heilmann, *Risk Watch: The Odds of Life* (New York: Facts on File Publications, 1984).

9

The Name Behind the Good News
(or *"The News Behind* His *Good Name"*)

Purpose

To promote a greater understanding of and appreciation for the sacredness of God's name.

Materials Needed

3" X 5" index cards, pencils
A book listing names and their meanings[1]

Preparation

As individuals enter, ask them to write their first name on a 3" X 5" index card. Have an assistant look up the meaning of that individual's name in the book mentioned above. Write the meaning of the name on the reverse side of the card. (If a name is not listed, and/or the person does not know the meaning of his or her name, have that individual write a "definition" that includes a distinguishing personality trait.) These will be used in "The Name Game" activity.

Introduction

Imagine living in a world where names are no longer used. Instead, for efficiency's sake, everything and everyone is assigned a number. For example, certain automobiles, computers, and even an occasional breakfast cereal are identified by a number instead of a name. But imagine asking for a date using digits:

"Hello, is this 27496? This is 83224. You don't know me, but you work with my best friend, 44328. He's asked 76581 to go to the symphony next Tuesday night, and he thought maybe you'd be interested in going as my date. You would? Great, 27496! I'll pick you up at seven."

Obviously, without a name there is something missing. There is a lack of emotion, a coldness that deadens the sense of anticipation.

A name helps give personal identity to an individual. To enhance this uniqueness, parents often choose a name which reflects some specific meaning. For example, some of the Puritan names from England were very descriptive. Among those found on a 1658 jury roll call were these: The-Gift-of-God Stringer, Joy-from-Above Brown, and Search-the-Scriptures Morton. And once, when a Puritan maiden was asked for her baptismal name, she replied: "Through-Much-Tribulation-We-Enter-the-Kingdom-of-Heaven, but for short they call me Tribby."

Fascinating. But we need not research published reports of intriguing names for there are some colorful "handles" close at hand.

Activity: "The Name Game"

Select one of the name cards filled out earlier. Give the meaning of the person's name aloud and have the audience attempt to guess whose name it describes. Do this for as many individuals as time allows. (Be sensitive to one who may feel self-conscious about an unusual name.)

This activity helps the group to become more familiar with the names of all members while developing the program theme.

Bridge

(The following should be presented in a light-hearted manner.) Depending on the embarrassment involved, some persons may feel that having their name's meaning exposed in public is "verbal abuse." Apologies from the management are hereby offered. Perhaps looking at the names of some well-known products, instead of people, will spare any further discomfort!

Thought Talk

Have you noticed how the brand names of certain products often become household terms? The technical term for this misuse of a trade name is called "eponomy." For example, seldom is a "photocopy" made. Rather, when students wish to duplicate notes, they make a "Xerox copy."

The brand name Xerox comes from the word *xerography*. This is the technical process which takes place in photocopying. Therefore, a true Xerox copy is made only on a machine bearing that name.

Another product name often used without thought is "Scotch Tape." In truth, there is just one genuine *Scotch Brand adhesive tape* which is manufactured by the 3M Company.

The story goes that this product gained its name from the fact that originally the adhesive was applied in thin strips only along the edges of the cellulose film. Dissatisfied customers contacted the manufacturer and suggested they not be so "Scotch" with their sticky stuff. The company got the message and the new version was called "Scotch tape." (Even if the story is an embellishment, it seems to have stuck.)

The list of eponomous names could go on: Jacuzzi, Jell-O, Kleenex, and many more. But there is another name which through the years has been more mistreated than perhaps all the others combined. It is not the name of a product, but rather the title of the One to whom we pray—God.

Bridge

Like the personal names we each have, God's name also has a meaning. But like thoughtlessly asking for a piece of "Scotch" tape to repair a torn "Xerox" copy, so God's name is often used without thinking.

Scripture contains various designations for God. As William Dyrness suggests, "God is personal in that he is the God who gives himself a name."[2]

Interestingly, each title for God found in the Bible reflects a certain characteristic about him and his relationship to his people.

Activity: Knowing His Name

Assign the following Bible texts to be read aloud:

1. Genesis 31:53
2. Genesis 17:1
3. Psalm 50:14
4. Genesis 16:13

5. Deuteronomy 3:24
6. Genesis 1:1
7. Psalm 24:7

After each passage is read, briefly explain the meaning of the title for God used within the verse. Following are some generally accepted definitions as rendered in the original Hebrew:[3]

1. Genesis 31:53—". . . the God of Abraham." *El.El.* Some believe this to be the oldest Semitic name for God. It means "mighty leader" or "governor" and stresses the distance between humanity and divinity. *El.El* also speaks of his power over the natural world.
2. Genesis 17:1—" . . . the Almighty God." *El Shaddai.* This title is a compound name using the previous designation, *El,* as a preface to *Shaddai.* The literal translation is unknown, although some scholars believe it could mean "God of the Mountains," referring to the mighty and exalted character of God.
3. Psalm 50:14—". . . fulfill your vows to the Most High." *Alion.* This name indicates the supreme position of God.
4. Genesis 16:13—"the God who sees me . . ." *El Roeh.* Again, a compound name. As the verse indicates, it refers to God's sovereign "sight," a watching over his earthly children.

5. Deuteronomy 3:24—"O Sovereign Lord . . ." *Yahweh.* Here is the name by which the Israelites knew God. It refers to his absolute, unchanging nature, and is connected with the covenant relationship. As such, it embraces the idea of nearness and concern for his chosen people.

Considering the speaking of God's name aloud as inappropriate, Jewish individuals do not pronounce the name *Yahweh.* For example, in reading the Scriptures aloud, *Adonai,* a word meaning "the Lord," is substituted for *Yahweh.* The mysterious title God instructed Abraham to refer to him as, "I am who I am" (Exodus 3:14), is also associated with the name *Yahweh.*

6. Genesis 1:1—"In the beginning God created . . ." *Elohim.* The name here may be interpreted two different ways. Some scholars feel that it points to the justice of God, while others believe it refers to the majesty of his Being.

7. Psalm 24:7—"the King of glory . . ." *Melek.* As the translation indicates, God is also seen as royalty, the One who reigns as king over all.

Ask the group members for other titles or names by which God is called, along with their meanings, if known.

"Knowing His Name" provides valuable information on the multi-dimensional aspects of God's name.

Application

God is known by many descriptive names in the Bible. But although his titles are varied, they undoubtedly capture only a small part of his unmatched glory and greatness.

In earlier Bible times, the mistreatment of God's name resulted in capital punishment. With Calvary, of course, came a new system of relating to divinity. But the sacredness ascribed to God's name did not lessen, nor has it since. Unfortunately, humans have taken advantage of the fact that blasphemy is not punishable by death. Taking God's name in vain has become a convenient means of bolstering one's self-image, as well as media ratings. As R. C. Sproul has written, "If the Old Testament laws were in effect today, every television network executive would have long ago been executed."[4]

Whatever the rationale underlying the abuse of God's name, spoken or unspoken, one thing is clear: He is not pleased with such profaning of his holiness. This is supported by one of the Ten Commandments: "You shall not misuse the name of the LORD your God, for the LORD will not hold anyone guiltless who misuses his name" (Exod. 20:7 NIV). In God's book, blasphemy is serious business.

What can we do to curb the trend? Here are some suggestions:

1. Beware the media's message. There is an advertising adage that says, "Repetition deepens effect." In other words, constant exposure to something increasingly embeds its message in our minds.

   The media allows and often seems to encourage the constant abuse of God's name. Remain sensitive to that fact and communicate your disapproval. Otherwise, blasphemy will continue to be seen as normal and right.

2. Know the character of God. Through the study of Scripture and other material, begin to get a firmer grip on who God really is and what he stands for. A deeper understanding of his divine attributes, particularly holiness, will result in a greater sense of reverence for God's name.

3. Affirm his holiness within relationships. Silence can speak loudly when it comes to God's holy name. Refuse to flippantly employ the name of God in casual conversation. In doing so, you will be quietly allowing others to see that he holds a very special place in your heart.

(If time allows, solicit further suggestions from group members.)

Wrap-up

Throughout history, those who have known God well have come to sense the sanctity surrounding his name. Likewise, all who stay in contact with their creator will develop a richer, deeper understanding of his character. They will come to see, indeed *sing,* as did King David: "Oh LORD, our Lord, how excellent is thy name . . ." (Psalm 8:1 KJV).

Discussion Questions

1. Why does God ask us to treat his name with respect?
2. What might be some reasons why people feel compelled to misuse God's name?
3. The Christian is encouraged to pray "in God's name." What does this mean?[5]
4. Reflecting on what God has meant personally to you, what would be a meaningful name/description of him? (Example: One who comforts, etc.)
5. You have a co-worker who considers himself a Christian. Nevertheless, he uses God's name on occasion to emphasize certain points during conversation. What would be an effective way to suggest that this is inappropriate?

Suggested Scripture

Exodus 20:7; Psalm 8:1; Matthew 6:9.

For Further Reading

Ronald B. Allen, *Moody Monthly,* October, 1989, pp. 38–43, "By His Name, His Nature" ("Digging Deeper" column).

R. C. Sproul, *The Holiness of God* (Wheaton, Ill.: Tyndale, 1985).

10

Trouble in Giver City
A Two-Segment Simulation Experience on Assisting the Needy

Purpose

To develop a policy in harmony with Christian principles for responding to individuals requesting assistance (i.e., food, money, clothing). The program is designed to be presented at two consecutive meetings.

Materials Needed

Paper, pencils
Lap-top computer or word processor, printer desirable
White board or newsprint, marker

Preparation

All of the cards found in the "Board Meeting Materials" section, along with the instructions for the "Pastor Wellsford Meets the McNeedys" skit, should be photocopied and distributed to selected individuals prior to the meeting. Give the participants a general idea of what the simulation experience will entail and their specific role in it. Also, the computer should be set up and ready for operation.

Introduction

Polished glass and colorful neon suggest that all is well in the marketplace. But back alleys and nearby park benches tell another story—a tale of homelessness and hopelessness.

The Bible clearly calls us to provide for those in need. Accordingly, many Christian organizations have devoted themselves to assisting not only street people, but also many other less fortunate ones. These ministries demonstrate their Christian commitment by supplying food, clothing, shelter, and other necessities. Those involved will indicate they are simply following the command to care for "the least of these" (Matt. 25:40).

Typically, the local church also attempts to reach out to those in need. Unfortunately, however, this caring body of believers often becomes the target of the unscrupulous and is preyed on because of Christian generosity. The resulting tragedy of such dishonesty is that those who are truly in need may be denied assistance.

The simulation experience, "Trouble in Giver City," is designed to help us work through the process of formulating a Christian "working policy" for responding to requests for assistance. Many opinions exist, and, while a solution may not easily surface, we'll gain a greater appreciation for the complexity often involved in assisting the needy.

Does a time ever come when a line must be drawn on Christian charity? Answering that question and furnishing guidelines for avoiding abuse in the realm of Christian generosity are what this program is all about.

Procedure

A. Skit—"Pastor Wellsford Meets the McNeedys"

Characters: Pastor Wellsford
               Mr. McNeedy
               Mrs. McNeedy
               Parishioner

The actors/actresses should have been informed previously of the basic plot and given at least a short time to discuss any details. A copy of the following may be furnished to the participants:

A destitute couple approaches the pastor of the Giver City Church in search of monetary assistance. The story line is flexible with the only requirement being that Pastor Wellsford makes the painful decision not to assist the couple due to insufficient "proof" of their need. This may be the result of a lack of credible references, or some other reason. A parishioner who has been waiting to speak with the pastor overhears the conversation and, after the McNeedys exit, proceeds to inform the pastor that he has not fulfilled his obligation as a Christian.

Unconvinced, Pastor Wellsford nevertheless agrees to bring up the matter of assisting the needy at the next board meeting.

B. Board Meeting Simulation

The leader indicates that the aforementioned "board meeting" is about to convene. The audience is informed that they are church members in attendance at the board meeting. Also, group members should be told that there may be some audience opinions shared which are merely being role-played (if *Position* cards were distributed beforehand). These individuals will be revealed at the appropriate time. At this point, those previously-selected board members and other participants now assume their various roles. The pastor, board members, and invited presenters take their places (preferably around a table). The pastor, also serving as board chairperson, informs the "attendees" of the problem which exists. He then introduces each invited presenter and the board members. Each presenter is then allowed to share briefly his/her position/perspective of the problem, along with a suggested solution. The board members are then asked to do the same.

C. Discussion

The board chairperson opens the floor for discussion of the problem of assisting the needy, soliciting comments and potential solutions from the audience.

Note: It is critical that the computer operator/s record specific relevant comments and suggestions from this point on.

During this time those individuals holding *Position* cards will share their perspective of the situation. After an ample period of discussion, indicate that the simulation portion of the program is over and move into the next segment. (Those holding Position cards may wish to be identified at this point and their real positions shared, if different from their prescribed role.)

D. Debrief

Prior to exploring the scriptural record on the topic of assisting those in need, it is important to briefly evaluate the previous experience. This may be done by asking the following questions:

1. Did the simulation generally reflect realistic concerns? In what area/s might it have been more authentic?
2. What were some of the strengths and weaknesses of the various perspectives/positions?
3. Was enough input supplied via the simulation to clearly portray the problem at hand? If not, what additional information would have helped?

(For further discussion, see Discussion Questions section.)

Explain that the main objective of the experience was to show the three-way tension that often exists between charity, responsibility, and vulnerability, along with the difficulty involved in arriving at a viable solution.

Wrap-up (for Part 1)

We've seen the problem and many perspectives. Now the challenge is to refine our ideals into a viable, Bible-based philosophy for meeting needs. We'll work on that very thing next time we're together.

"Trouble in Giver City" Simulation: Part 2

E. Biblical Perspective

After briefly reviewing Part 1, begin with the following:

The importance of assisting those in need is a major theme of Scripture. Perhaps the classic passage relating to Christian caring is found in Matthew 25:31–40. It's the first section of Jesus' parable of the sheep and goats:

> When the Son of Man comes in his glory, and all the angels with him, he will sit on his throne in heavenly glory. All the nations will be gathered before him, and he will separate the people one from another as a shepherd separates the sheep from the goats. He will put the sheep on his right and the goats on his left.
>
> Then the King will say to those on his right, "Come, you who are blessed by my Father; take your inheritance, the kingdom prepared for you since the creation of the world. For I was hungry and you gave me something to eat, I was thirsty and you gave me something to drink, I was a stranger and you invited me in, I needed clothes and you clothed me, I was sick and you looked after me, I was in prison and you came to visit me."
>
> Then the righteous will answer him, "Lord, when did we see you hungry and feed you, or thirsty and give you something to drink? When did we see you a stranger and invite you in, or needing clothes and clothe you? When did we see you sick or in prison and go to visit you?"
>
> The King will reply, "I tell you the truth, whatever you did for one of the least of these brothers of mine, you did for me."

Caring for others has become a natural response to God's indwelling. But another side must be considered: the intriguing admonition in Matthew 10:16. Here Jesus is preparing the twelve disciples to take their message of redemption on the road. In so doing, he says, "I am sending you out like sheep among wolves. Therefore, *be as shrewd as snakes and as innocent as doves.*"

Such counsel may be appropriate for not only dealing with local councils and those in the "synagogue," but perhaps also when responding to potential recipients of Christian charity.

F. Needs Evaluation Document

This section of the program is designed to result in a simple set of guidelines to help concerned Christians be both selfless yet savvy in their giving to others.

The computer operator should now read aloud the basic concerns, along with comments and suggestions, which surfaced during the discussion segment of the program. (It is helpful if this data was organized and printed out, with photocopies being furnished to the group members.) Using this information, along with the biblical insight just given and audience interaction, write on the white board a sequential method for responding to requests for assistance by individuals apparently in need. While a general statement of philosophy may be formed, the policy should also include (1) a sensitive method of evaluating needs, and (2) appropriate response/s to specific concerns, such as where the most effective form of ministry lies (church, social service agency). Other concerns may also be addressed.

The computer operator should enter and save the finalized document information. This may be printed out, photocopied, and distributed the following week. It may also be appropriate to supply a copy to the pastor for consideration.

Wrap-up

Scripture is clear: the Christian must provide for those in need. But the Bible also leaves no doubt as to the value of exercising good judgment in all matters.

Because every situation is unique, a blanket policy on caring for the needy is insufficient. Accordingly, any request for assistance must be considered on an individual basis. The purpose of a bonafide set of guidelines to assist in that task is not merely to "sift out" the unscrupulous. More importantly, it helps assure that a legitimate need will not go unmet.

The contemporary disciple faces a significant challenge in the realm of charity: the crossing of compassion for those whose earthly inventory is low, with wisdom from on high. Such a hybrid can be grown in only one place: the greenhouse of God's grace. And the prayer of each "gardener" must be that the fruit produced might reflect his ultimate will.

Board Meeting Materials

Character cards

Invited presenters:

Presenter #1: _____, director of Caring Heart Center for the Needy. Your concern for the less fortunate comes primarily from a position of *moral,* not religious, obligation. You subscribe to a philosophy of helping those who attempt to help themselves. Accordingly, your organization assists in the process of job placement.

A significant factor in Caring Heart's limited ability to assist the needy is the lack of both physical space and funds. You see increased governmental responsibility for caring for the needy as the most viable solution to easing the burden of private organizations.

Presenter #2: _____, assistant director of the city's social services agency. Your position on assisting the needy reflects the reality that inadequate government funding for those in need severely limits your agency's ability to adequately meet the demand for assistance. While genuinely concerned for the less fortunate, you believe the ultimate solution is for churches and parachurch organizations to increasingly assume more of the responsibility for caring for the needy.

Presenter #3: _____, local citizen. You represent a strong faction of upper-income community members who perceive local taxation to already unjustly favor the poor. The corporate position of this group is a "survival of the fittest" concept, with sociological "natural selection" an effective control to assure just distribution of wealth and material goods.

Board member cards

Pastor Wellsford. As the senior pastor (and board chairperson) of the Giver City Community Church, you are besieged with requests for assistance. Your Christian belief in helping the poor is currently in tension with the fact that many of the church's welfare funds have been unwittingly distributed to professional panhandlers, etc. Nevertheless, you remain committed to the idea of reaching out to those in need.

Board Member #1. You are vehemently opposed to any form of unreciprocated assistance. Your attitude is that anyone who is willing to work hard can find gainful employment and should thankfully do so.

Board Member #2. You believe that concerning requests from the needy for financial assistance, it is not for another human being to judge the validity of that person's claims. You feel that Scripture indicates an attitude of unconditional caring, thereby disallowing any form of discrimination such as a "screening" process to evaluate one's needs.

Board Member #3. You are of the opinion that contributing financially to organizations equipped to handle the needs of the less fortunate is the wisest choice for the Christian in today's uncertain world. This assures that funds will be used in the most efficient manner possible and avoids the myriad difficulties surrounding "on site" requests for assistance.

Position cards

Position #1. You believe that what life has robbed the unfortunate of should be supplied by those who are most able to furnish it (the wealthy).

Position #2. You believe only those who are willing to work should be rewarded. However, your position also holds that reimbursement should be in the form of "necessities" rather than cash. This, in your opinion, will help avoid the possibility that the work arrangement is simply helping to support a vice or inappropriate lifestyle.

Position #3. You believe that government, local and federal, is primarily responsible for providing for the needy. The church's responsibility begins only when various social service agencies have been depleted of their resources.

Position #4. You believe that the church is primarily responsible for caring for those in need. Only when funds or other barriers prevent proper ministry to the unfortunate from taking place should government be called on for assistance.

Discussion Questions

1. Are the wealthy more obligated to provide for the needy than are those of lesser income? Why/why not?

2. What should be the "tangible" response on the part of the individual receiving charity?
3. Does the overall ministry of Jesus reflect any degree of selectivity in providing for the needs of others? If so, in what way/s? If not, how does his example work in today's world?
4. Agree/disagree: the capitalist philosophy is intrinsically wrong because it fosters inequality between the rich and poor. (Opinions should be supported.)
5. It has been shown that some "street people" are content with their lifestyle. What should be the attitude of the Christian toward such individuals?

Suggested Scripture

Exodus 22:25–27; Deuteronomy 15:1–11; Proverbs 19:17; Matthew 7:1, 10:16, 25:31–46; James 2:15–17.

For Further Reading

Robert G. Clouse, editor, *Wealth and Poverty* (Downers Grove, Ill.: Inter-Varsity Press, 1984).

Donald B. Kraybill, *The Upside-Down Kingdom* (Scottdale, Penn.: Herald Press, 1978).

11

To Tell the Truth

Purpose

To learn how to effectively apply eternal principles of love and honesty to truth-telling (and other) situations requiring ethical choice. For college-age/young adult groups, Dr. Norman Geisler's theory of graded absolutism is explored.

Materials Needed

Pencils, 3" X 5" cards

Preparation

If the optional activity, "A Tale of Two Tribesmen" is used, it will be necessary to photocopy the exercise for participants.

Introduction

"The truth and nothing but the truth." Living by that ethical creed should be second nature to every Christian. But because sin has touched human existence, we face decisions we wish could be avoided. The once cut-and-dried has become hazy, and complex questions have no simple answers.

One area that has caused distress in all ages is truth-telling. While the situations change, a basic question remains: Are there rare times when honesty may not be the best policy? That's something we're going to soon consider. But first, a little fun!

Activity: "To Tell the Truth" Game

This exercise is based on the 1960s television program of the same name. Distribute an index card and pencil to members as they enter. Ask each individual to write down his or her name and a personal characteristic or event which no one else in the group is likely to be aware of. This might be an embarrassing moment, personal triumph, or any other singular experience. Collect the cards and select *one* experience to be used during the first round of play. Ask the person whose experience is being used and two other individuals to step into another room. The three are then informed of the experience selected, and a phrase of introduction to be used at the beginning of play is agreed on. For example, if the real person was once expelled from school, the common introduction spoken by each contestant in turn could be "I was once expelled from school." On returning, each person introduces himself or herself using the identical phrase, then sits down facing the audience. The audience must determine who actually belongs to the situation by asking probing questions. (Asking directly if it is a certain contestant is not allowed.) The actual person tells the truth, while the imposters respond as if they were the real person, making up details as necessary. After a given time or number of questions, the audience is asked to vote according to whom they believe is telling the truth. Finally, the moderator asks of the three, "Will the real person who was once expelled from school (or other situation) please stand up?" After all feign standing, the actual person finally rises.

As used here, "To Tell the Truth" serves two purposes. First, it allows participants to learn more about each other. It also sets the tone for the ensuing look into the subject of truth-telling.

Bridge

Any "To Tell the Truth" contestant has been issued a temporary license to lie. But real life is hardly a game show. And yet, because of its complexity, life holds ethical dilemmas; whether or not to conceal the truth can be one of those.

Christians must base moral decisions (which include truth-telling) on something deeper than today's horoscope. Certainly sound principles are necessary, and theories can prove helpful. But history has shown that morality in decision-making cannot ultimately be legislated for or dictated to another.

As creatures of free will we must make choices. To what extent this freedom can be exercised in good conscience has been a matter of debate in Christian circles. Those who subscribe to the philosophy of "situation ethics" believe that love is the ultimate principle on which ethical decisions must be made. But who defines what love is in a specific situation?

Others are certain that prayer can provide the right solution to an ethical question. But praying fervently while deciding whether or not to tell a mugger about the $100 bill in your right sock would be quite a spiritual feat!

Still another group believes that ethical conflicts simply do not exist within the framework of God's sovereign will. Rather, the sinful human condition merely causes us to perceive a given situation as a moral dilemma.

Fortunately, Scripture provides some significant insight concerning tough, "ethically-nebulous" situations which demand an immediate decision. But before considering the Bible's viewpoint, let's set the stage with a practical example of ethical tension.

Discussion: "Between a Rock and Hard Disk"

Present the following situation to the audience: For the past two years you have been employed by IBX Business Systems as a word processor. During this time, a close friendship has developed between you and a co-worker who is a single parent. You have learned that your friend's child has been diagnosed as having a rare disease which, left untreated, will prove fatal.

Although there is a strict policy regarding the use of company equipment for personal gain, you have become aware that your friend has been doing this very thing to help pay off mounting expenses related to her child's situation.

One day, your supervisor discovers onscreen the remnants of one of your friend's freelance word processing jobs. She turns to you and asks, "Do you know who is responsible for this?" A "yes" will likely result in your friend losing her job, but replying "no" would be concealing the truth. (*To the audience.*) How would you respond, and why? (Allow for a brief discussion.)

Biblical Perspective

The Bible gives us no word on freelance word processing. But it does contain several intriguing examples of individuals facing an ethical dilemma involving truth-telling. The first chapter of Exodus is a good example. Here, the Hebrew midwives must choose between telling the truth and allowing the death of thousands of innocent children, or lying and saving their lives:

> The king of Egypt said to the Hebrew midwives, whose names were Shiphrah and Puah, "When you help the Hebrew women in childbirth and observe them on the delivery stool, if it is a boy, kill him; but if it is a girl, let her live." The midwives, however, feared God and did not do what the king of Egypt had told them to do; they let the boys live. Then the king of Egypt summoned the midwives and asked them, "Why have you done this? Why have you let the boys live?" The midwives answered Pharoah, "Hebrew women are not like Egyptian women, they are vigorous and give birth before the midwives arrive" (Exod. 1:15–19).

The lie is elected, and the children live. What is Scripture's response to this decision that seems so discordant with other biblical commands (i.e., Exod. 20:16, Prov. 12:22, Eph. 4:25, etc.)? Again, the record is clear: "So God was kind to the midwives and the people increased and became even more numerous. And because the midwives feared God, he gave them families of their own" (Exod. 1:20–21).

Thought Talk*

It is perplexing, indeed disturbing, for some people to discover that God could affirm an action which seems directly opposed to his moral will. But in his book *Options in Contemporary Chris-*

---

*This discussion would work best in a young adult or college-age group setting.

tian Ethics[1], Dr. Norman Geisler suggests why it may sometimes be so.

Graded absolutism is a system of ethics based on three primary premises: First, there are higher and lower moral laws; second, unavoidable moral conflicts do exist; and third, no guilt is imputed to us for the unavoidable.

Among the many Scripture passages quoted in support of the idea that not all moral laws are of equal weight is Matthew 23:23. There Jesus refers to the weightier matters of the law. Also cited are Matthew 5:19 and 22:36, where the least and the greatest commandments are mentioned. Geisler's thought is that because of the sinful reality of moral conflicts, we are required to choose the higher moral law in certain situations. In the case of the Hebrew midwives, the moral law of mercy took precedence over the moral law of truth-telling. Geisler believes that, having made their decision on such a basis, it warranted no guilt. He writes, "God does not hold the individual responsible for personally unavoidable moral conflicts, providing they keep the higher law."[2] As a result, the author suggests that "Graded absolutism releases given human actions from the legalistic clutches of a necessary association with evil."[3]

Geisler is quick to point out the difference between "situation ethics" and graded absolutism when he says, "First, [situation ethics] does not believe there are any contentful absolutes; graded absolutism does."[4] Elsewhere he writes, "In situation ethics (such as Joseph Fletcher's), the circumstances determine what is right and what is wrong. For the graded absolutist, however, the situation does not determine what is right; it merely helps us discover which absolute moral principle applies."[5]

Is there a place for sanctified falsifying? The theory of graded absolutism would make it seem so. But is the theory a plausible one?

React/Respond

Ask participants to respond to the question of why or why not the theory of graded absolutism is viable. (See discussion questions.) Discussion of alternative theories may be appropriate. Also, application of theories to various hypothetical ethical dilemmas, including the situation previously described in "Between a Rock and a Hard Disk," could prove enlightening.

Wrap-up

It would perhaps take divine intervention to arrive at a consensus regarding ethics in *any* situation, including truth-telling. Fortunately for most individuals, situations involving moral conflict are not the norm. But even amid the haze of human dilemmas such as we've discussed, one thing remains clear: whatever ethical choices we make must be based on the eternal principles found in God's Word. Heaven will appreciate the fact that our decisions were made with more than mere human ideas in mind.

Discussion Questions

1. Some people would suggest that "good intentions" automatically absolve any moral guilt which may be associated with ethical conflict and decision-making. Is this correct? Why/why not?
2. Are there degrees of truth? If so, how would these categories be defined? (Some possible headings: Facticity, Enhancement, Deterrent, Embellishment, Deception.)
3. What is the difference between Christianity and morality? In ethical decision-making are the results the same for both? Why/why not?
4. In one sentence, define the point at which truth becomes a lie.
5. Geisler speaks of two alternatives to graded absolutism. The first is what he calls unqualified absolutism, which suggests that moral conflicts are only apparent, and therefore sin is always avoidable in them. The other option is termed conflicting absolutism, which says that moral conflicts do exist, but guilt (albeit forgivable) always accompanies any attempt to resolve these conflicts. What are the strengths and weaknesses of each of these views?

Suggested Scripture

Joshua 2:1–7, 6:17; Proverbs 19:5; Micah 6:8.

For Further Reading

William Barclay, *Ethics in a Permissive Society* (New York: Harper & Row, 1971).

Joseph Fletcher, *Situation Ethics* (Philadelphia: The Westminster Press, 1966).

Norman Geisler, *Options in Contemporary Christian Ethics* (Grand Rapids: Baker, 1981).

12

Exercise Your Faith

Purpose

To show the centrality of the person of Jesus Christ in the experience of faith. James Fowler's study of faith development is presented.

Materials Needed

None

Introduction

"If only I had more faith." How many have been led to believe that quantity of belief is the key ingredient in reaping spiritual results! Such a perspective reminds one of Lewis Carroll's White Queen, who speaks to Alice in *Through the Looking Glass:*

> "I can't believe *that!*" said Alice.
> "Can't you?" the Queen said in a pitying tone. "Try again: draw a long breath, and shut your eyes."
> Alice laughed. "There's no use trying," she said, "one can't believe impossible things."
> "I daresay you haven't much practice," said the Queen. "When I was your age, I always did it for half-an-hour a day. Why, some-

times I've believed as many as six impossible things before breakfast."[1]

Without question, the Bible indicates that faith *is* an important part of the Christian experience. Scripture also shows that there is a connection between faith and the miraculous. But it is a narrow view which sees faith primarily as a spiritual muscle to be flexed in quest of the sensational. Rather, a richer, more mature perspective of faith comes when the focus shifts from *results* to a *relationship*.

Story: "Faith-ercise"

Willard Newson, recent convert, cheerily entered the sporting goods store at the local mall.

"How can I help you today?" an athletic-looking salesclerk inquired.

"I'm here to pick out a few items so I can begin exercising my faith," Willard explained. The salesperson lifted an eyebrow as Willard retrieved a list from his jacket pocket.

"The first thing I'll need," he said, perusing the list, "is a helmet. I want to protect my head from rocks rolling down the sides of the mountains I'll soon be moving."

The salesclerk stifled a snicker. "I believe you mean *climbing,*" he said.

"Well, that's a possibility, too," Willard replied. "But I can use the same helmet for both. So, where are they?" he asked, looking around.

The confused clerk hesitated, eyeing Willard suspiciously. Nevertheless, he led the way past the fishing rods and hunting jackets over to the mountain-climbing gear.

After selecting an attractive earthtone helmet, Willard again spoke to the clerk. "Next I'd like to see the swimwear," he said.

Just how a bathing suit would afford much defense against a rockslide the clerk could not fathom. But he showed Willard the available styles.

"This looks like a modest choice," Willard commented, considering a blue knee-length suit. "Not that I'll need it for long.

But I'm bound to go under at least a time or two before I get the hang of walking on water."

At this, the salesclerk considered dialing mall security. But Willard's next request cut short this idea.

"The last thing I'll need to have a look at is your camping gear," he said. "Once my faith is in shape, I'm bound to be swamped with requests—financial security, health, and happiness, that sort of thing. The locals won't be a problem, but I thought I'd pitch a few pup tents on the front lawn for the overnighters."

Bewildered, the salesperson once again paraded through the store, halting amid cookstoves, backpacks, and other outdoor items. Without speaking, he pointed to the tents. A quick "about face," and the perplexed salesclerk headed off in the opposite direction, muttering something about applying for work at the adjacent health food store, where at least the nuts didn't talk.

Shortly, Willard had selected several complementary tent styles which he would tastefully arrange around the new highlight of his landscaped yard—a recently-installed electric fountain which he called "Old Faithful."

Willard paid for his purchases and arranged for delivery of the tents. He hurried out the door. His last stop before beginning to exercise his faith was to be the Happy Hoe Garden Center. He still lacked a supply of mustard seeds.

Just as he reached the mall exit, Willard caught sight of a sign he had not noticed before. It read: "Son Power Spiritual Fitness Center." Could providence be at work? Until now, he had been planning to exercise his faith at home, following the routine of a well-known television faith-erciser. But think of the high-tech equipment a professional training center must have: water-walking practice jacuzzis, electronic monitoring of faith-to-doubt ratio, and computerized speedbag simulators for fighting the good fight. This would be faith-ercising at its finest! Excited over the possibility, Willard headed over to sign up. Swinging open the narrow door he stepped inside.

But to his surprise, the long room was empty! There was no equipment in sight! The only sign of life was a stream of light pouring through the cracks of a door at the far end of the room.

Just then, the distant door opened, and out stepped a gentleman dressed in white. He walked toward Willard. Sensing his confusion, the man spoke.

"You're undoubtedly here to exercise your faith." He held out his hand. "Welcome. I'm Gabe de Angelo, the assistant trainer."

Willard hesitantly shook the man's hand. "Uh, nice to meet you," he said. Then, hoping to satisfy his curiosity, he commented, "I guess your rates must be pretty low here, since you don't seem to have much of anything to offer your clients."

Gabe smiled. "Well, the truth is we don't charge anything. As for the lack of exercise equipment, experience has shown that it's more of a hindrance than a help when it comes to achieving strong faith."

"I don't know," Willard protested. "With no training equipment, how can a faith rookie like me ever hope to become a big-time believer?" He then added, "Frankly, I'm not sure your way of exercising faith would even be worth trying."

Gabe de Angelo placed a hand on Willard's shoulder. Looking him straight in the eye, he said, "Willard, our way is the only way. Once you're into the program, you'll begin to see that strong faith is not the result of trying. Rather, it comes by trusting in our instructor and becoming more like him."

A strange sense of conviction began to grow within Willard. After a brief silence, he cleared his throat and spoke.

"I'd like to meet your instructor," he said.

"Follow me," came the quick reply. Gabe led Willard to the little room behind the door of which the bright light still shone. "Go on in, Willard. There are some others who came today, too. But the instructor has been waiting for you. He said he didn't want to begin without you."

A quizzical look crossed Willard's face. "But how . . ." Gabe cut Willard's question short.

"Once you get to know him better," he said, a twinkle in his eye, "you'll understand."

For some reason, Willard believed him. He went into the room and sat down. It was to be the first of many evenings spent working out under the guidance of the instructor.

To date, Willard hasn't moved Mt. Everest or walked across Lake Tahoe. He hasn't had any calls for cures or cash either. But if you ask him how his exercise program is going, he'll tell you he's certain that his faith is getting stronger every day.

Bridge

Faith is a fascinating topic. Let's find out more about what *we* believe.

Activity: "Belief Ballots"

This activity is designed to creatively elicit reflection and response concerning concepts found in the story "Faith-ercise." More general thoughts on the topic of faith are also presented for participants' reaction.

Designate three separate areas of the room as follows: one area is for those who *agree,* a second for *possibly,* and a third area for individuals who *disagree.* After each of the following statements on faith is read, have individuals move to the area which most accurately reflects his or her opinion regarding it. After each "vote" has been taken, ask (at random) for participants to tell why they moved as they did. (Tip: those who make up the smallest areas after each vote often have more definitive and colorful comments than the others.)

Questions for "Belief Ballots"

1. The essence of faith is more process than product.
2. A growing faith is an inevitable result of communion with Christ.
3. Faith, trust, and belief are different words describing the same thing. (Encourage definitions for each word, assuming some persons have disagreed.)
4. Faith in Christ is a purely spiritual matter.
5. True Christian faith will always be manifested by tangible evidence (see James 2:17).
6. "Life asks no questions that faith cannot answer."
7. Prayer + Faith = Power

Biblical Perspective

The Bible clearly indicates that faith is the mainstay of the Christian experience. The believer is encouraged by the fact that "through Christ, all things are possible." But faith must be based on more than the miraculous. Scripture makes it clear that a mature, growing faith is rooted in a relationship with the redeemer.

The eleventh and twelfth chapters of Hebrews contain significant insight regarding the issue of faith. Verse one of chapter eleven sets forth this definition:

> Now faith is being sure
> of what we hope for
> and certain
> of what we do not see.

At first glance, one might be led to the conclusion that the believer is asked to place his or her confidence in something for which there is no tangible evidence. The passage, however, reeks of conviction, as the words *sure* and *certain* suggest.

C. S. Lewis is helpful in providing a definition of faith that shows clearly the blending of the empirical with the intangible. He writes, "Faith is the art of holding on to things your reason has accepted as true, in spite of your changing moods."[2]

In a thought which relates to the logic of a person's faith, someone has said: "One's faith is only as good as the object in which it is placed."

The author of Hebrews has synthesized all of the above (and more) definitions of faith. He would have us know that while there is an element of the unseen involved, the Christian's faith is based on a series of well-grounded facts: that God became man, lived among us, died, and rose from the grave. That is why, following a listing of some of history's great men and women of faith, Hebrews 12:2 turns to faith's focal point: "Let us fix our eyes on Jesus, the author and perfecter of our faith. . . ."

Personal Application*

Thomas Droege, in his book *Faith Passages and Patterns*, refers to a study which provides insight concerning the broader, ongoing journey of faith.[3]

The study, done by James Fowler, is patterned somewhat after Jean Piaget's stages of mental development and Lawrence Kohlberg's stages of moral development. As the result of his empirical studies, Fowler suggests that there are six basic stages of faith development. The levels are reached in a step-by-step process, yet at certain times individuals may revert to previous stages. Fowler's six primary stages are: (encourage audience members to consider in the light of this study where they should be in their faith journey.)

Stage 1: "God's just like my mommy and daddy."
Children from the ages of two to six come to think of God in the same way they view their parents. Images of God do not fit into a cohesive pattern, but children shape the necessary pieces into a framework which fits their needs.

Stage 2: "What's fair is fair!"
Justice is a central issue for those between the ages of seven to twelve. Stories are important, with the "good guy" winning out in the end the only acceptable option. As a result, the concept of grace (for the "bad guy") can be difficult to grasp.

Stage 3: "I believe what the church believes."
This faith stage typically involves approximately ages thirteen to eighteen. It is a period of extreme self-consciousness. Accordingly, these individuals are significantly influenced by others' expectations and judgments of them, perceived or otherwise. Indoctrination is effective, but only with great difficulty do believers in Stage 3 communicate why they believe what they do. According to Fowler, many Christians remain in Stage 3 throughout their entire lives.

Stage 4: "As I see it, God is . . ."
Here is a stage of critical thinking and new ideas about God. How one thinks about God becomes important, not merely the con-

*This discussion would work best in a young adult or college-age group setting.

tent of one's faith. It is a time of intellectualizing which, according to Fowler, may carry with it as much loss as gain. Yet, it is necessary to have reached this stage if one's faith is to continue to grow toward its ultimate goal.

Stage 5: "Don't confuse the map with the territory." Stage 4 thinkers are concerned with having matters of faith "mapped out" as it were, with boundaries in place for the predictable journey. But those who have reached Stage 5 have come to sense that there is much to faith that can never be empirically known, hence they develop a growing appreciation for mystery. Sacraments and other symbols of faith take on new meaning. Stage 5 believers are also very open to dialog and are willing to view faith from new perspectives. Such is a maturity that comes by knowing God deeply and resting securely in his love.

Stage 6: "I have a dream." According to Fowler, the ultimate faith-stage is attained by very few. Using the phrase from Martin Luther King, Jr.'s famous civil rights speech, these "dreamers" are those who live out their lives in a quest to see the dream of the Kingdom of God fully realized. To live in peace and harmony with one another, and represent God on earth is the call which these have heeded.

In conclusion, author Droege asks the question: Is one stage better than another? He answers by pointing out that if a greater sense of worthiness in God's eyes is being sought, then no, a succeeding stage is not better than a previous one. But, he adds, if one is striving for a more mature, self-fulfilling faith, then yes, reaching a higher stage of faith is better than existing at a lower one.

Wrap-up

Regardless of where one may be in his or her spiritual journey, it is important to remember the true source of abiding faith. Faith spurts may occasionally come to the Christian, and miracles actually occur. But it is through consistent contact with Christ that a mature faith evolves.

Feeling weak in the realm of belief? There is no better time than the present to fall to your knees and begin to exercise your faith!

Discussion Questions

1. Why does God sometimes seem to delay responding to requests made "in faith"?
2. Is it possible to exercise one's faith on a regular basis? If so, how might this be done?
3. Define and discuss the differences between faith and presumption.
4. How does Christian faith differ from secular faith (faith in oneself, another person, or institution)?
5. Some people would attribute a mountain-moving experience to fortunate timing rather than divine intervention. Convinced of heaven's role in such an experience, how might such a conviction be best communicated to the nonbeliever?

Suggested Scripture

Habakkuk 2:4; Matthew 17:14-21; Mark 9:38–40; 2 Corinthians 5:7; Hebrews 11:1–12:2.

For Further Reading

Thomas A. Droege, *Faith Passages and Patterns* (Philadelphia: Fortress Press, 1983).

W. Bingham Hunter, *The God Who Hears* (Downers Grove, Ill.: Inter-Varsity Press, 1986), chapter 12, "Believing: The Prayer of Faith."

C. S. Lewis, *Mere Christianity* (New York: Macmillan, 1943), chapters 11 and 12, "Faith."

13

No More Closet Creativity

Purpose

To encourage development of God's gift of creativity.

Materials Needed

Pencils, paper for all
White board or newsprint, marker

Preparation

Type or write on a piece of paper the following: "Life is like _____: _____."
Photocopy enough for each participant to receive one. These will be used in the activity "Life Is Like . . ."

Introduction

Murray Spengler was a department store janitor whose responsibilities included sweeping the long wooden aisles.

Murray, distressed at the inefficiency of the conventional broom and miserable because his asthma condition was aggravated by the resulting dust, thought surely there must be a better way to clean the store's floors. The wheels of creativity began to spin.

Soon Spengler designed a crude contraption, using a fan and his wife's pillowcase. It actually sucked up dirt from the floor! The device was faster and more effective than a broom. Murray felt his new-fangled grit-grabber might just prove to be the floor-sweeper of the future.

But the inventive janitor knew that his product could benefit others only by having it put into production. Murray himself, however, lacked the needed capital. But he *did* know of someone else whose cash flow was greater than his own. A meeting was arranged. The man recognized the massive potential of Murray's creation and agreed to sponsor its production.

You guessed it. Murray Spengler's brainchild, the vacuum cleaner, was destined for a glorious future. And Murray's investor, a man whose last name happened to be Hoover, would also clean up as the business continued to grow.

The "Hoover" logo on upright and canister models today is really a tribute to store janitor Murray Spengler. Our lives are made a little easier because he claimed the gift of "creativity."

Bridge

Who comes to mind when you think of a creative person? Michelangelo? Emily Dickinson? Picasso? (If desired, also allow for audience response.)

These individuals were certainly gifted with creativity. Indeed, every person has been given the ability to create. Of course, we do not create *ex nihilo,* or "out of nothing," as God does, but we are still meant to experience the joy of self-expression through creative acts. Creativity is a gift of God.

Nevertheless, it's still hard for some people to believe that they can be creative. So to demonstrate our creativity, let's try a little exercise. It's time to bring our gift of creativity out of the closet!

Activity: "Life Is Like . . ."

Distribute pencil and a prepared "Life Is Like" slip (as noted in "Preparation" section) to each person. Have them complete the phrase "Life is like a _____." They should then furnish another sentence of explanation. An example might be, "Life is like a *country road. The ride isn't always the smoothest, but if you stick with it, it'll take you where you need to go.*" Encourage creativity! (Instrumental background music is helpful.)

After a few (2–3) minutes, have group members read aloud their newly-created metaphors.

"Life Is Like . . ." is a simple way to allow individuals to express themselves creatively. These phrases can also indicate the way various persons really do view life! This background information can be helpful when ministering to specific individuals.

Bridge

Too often, we view creativity as something reserved for the avant-garde, "off-the-wall" individual. Creativity, however, does not equal eccentricity. Rather, creativity is an expression of oneself that reflects God's personal, unique gifts to that person. To whose glory we use our creativity is another matter.

Typically, we may not think of Jesus as unusually creative. But in an article in *Discipleship Journal* magazine, Sue Monk Kidd captures several colorful pictures of the creative Christ. Throughout his ministry, Jesus often refused to conform to meaningless, ministry-restricting tradition. As the author points out, "Jesus related to people in a way that broke down tradition and opened doors to creative encounters."[1]

We're going to look at some ways that we might use our best creative efforts to God's glory. But first, let's quickly look at a few of the rewards of nurturing our God-given creativity.

Biblical Perspective

While the reasons for becoming a more creative person are many, some basic incentives include: (These should be listed on a white board or newsprint.)

1. Personal expression. There are times when a creative act can say something in a way which otherwise would lose its

intensity. That's why a forgiven woman once poured spike-nard over the Savior's feet. The effect of this creative act? Jesus stated it clearly: "I tell you the truth, wherever the gospel is preached throughout the world, what she has done will also be told . . ." (Mark 14:9).

2. Personal satisfaction and enrichment. The first chapter of the Bible portrays God as becoming increasingly satisfied with his creative efforts. Early acts of creation are called "good" (Gen. 1:10, 12, etc.), but by the sixth day the joy is even greater. Now the splendor is called "very good" (Gen. 1:31). Just as God "sighed" with satisfaction, so may we enjoy the fruits and fulfillment of our creative labors.

3. Ministry value. No one was more creative in ministry than Jesus: parables rich with meaning; personal encounters that broke religious, traditional, and ethnic boundaries. Jesus made ministry happen—in places as colorful as beside a well and in a fishing boat. Creativity was one of his key ingredients to effective ministry. So it can be for us.

4. Spiritual growth. No one knew better the lasting effects of creative expression than King David. Music and poetry would at different times serve as avenues of both comfort and recommitment. His creativity would last a lifetime, as Psalm 146:2 suggests: "I will praise the LORD all my life; I will sing praise to my God as long as I live." Creativity can help us keep in tune with the Creator.

5. Witness value. In today's fast-paced world, creative solutions to complex problems are in high demand. By providing creative, honest answers to this world's questions, the Christian glorifies God as the ultimate source of solutions (see James 1:17).

Bridge

Throughout history there have been many great creative acts. The pyramids of Egypt, the Mona Lisa, the airplane, and the pacemaker are just a few.

But what of the creativity of God? What are some of his most significant expressions of creativity—past and present?

Activity: "Crown Creation"

Solicit at random audience members' responses as to what they perceive as being God's greatest expressions of creativity. Then read the following aloud (you may wish to have this written on an index card): In his book, *Knowing the Face of God,* author Tim Stafford makes this assertion: "[God's] most creative and painstaking work is the church, the body of Christ . . . it is his beloved project."[2]

Next, have participants vote (by raising hands) according to whether they (1) agree or (2) disagree with the author's idea that God's most creative work is in fact "the church." After the voting has taken place, ask various group members to tell why they voted as they did.

Follow-up questions might include (1) Are God's creative acts different from his creative work? If so, how? (2) Do we have a role to play in either of these? If so, what might it be?

"Crown Creation" is a good lead-in to demonstrate how the contemporary disciple can participate in the creative work of redemption.

Bridge

Certainly creation reflects God's creative power. But Tim Stafford writes,

> God's work is more than nature. He barely began there. People generally concede that you can know something about God through the universe he has made: "The heavens are telling the glory of God." But . . . God does not love stars as he loves me. The heavens, for all their splendor, will outlive their usefulness; they will be rolled up and taken away. So will the world we live in, for all its sensual glory and intricate ecology. They are like the scaffolding that Michelangelo designed for painting the Sistine Chapel—marvelous in its own right, but dismantled at the proper time so that the great work could be clearly seen. When God had created everything else he went on to man and woman, creatures who sat up and talked to each other, who talked to him. He has been working to complete these creatures ever since. He even

became one. His people are God's great work, to be displayed in an entirely new setting—a new heaven and a new earth.[3]

Wrap-up

Creativity is an avenue to personal fulfillment and a resource to help meet the everyday challenges of life; but it is also a vital tool of the heavenly "trade" of redemption. As Christians, we are called to be God's instruments in drawing the distracted to Jesus with thoughtful imagination.

Why not begin stretching yourself for the sake of the gospel? Turn your creativity on for God. As Murray Spengler learned, your dream can make a difference.

Discussion Questions

1. In the arts, the term *creative expression* is sometimes used in defense of overt sensuality, etc. For the Christian, what delineates true creative expression from artistic abuse?
2. What are some examples of creative expression found in Scripture?
3. You have just encountered a salty dock-worker who ridicules your belief in God by saying it's foolish to "talk to someone who never talks back, and believe in someone you've never seen." What is the most creative response you can think of to these objections?
4. What are some specific ways a person might practice becoming more creative?
5. Creativity is an important ingredient in effective ministry. Give imaginative ideas for reaching out to others, and/or the personal and corporate worship experience.

Suggested Scripture

Genesis 1:1, 27, 2:19, 20; The Parables of Jesus;
1 Corinthians 12:4–11.

For Further Reading

Werner Kirst and Ulrich Diekmeyer, *Creativity Training: Become Creative in 30 Minutes a Day* (New York: Peter H. Wyden, 1973).

Gerard I. Nierenberg, *The Art of Creative Thinking* (New York: Simon & Schuster, 1982).

Robert W. Olson, *The Art of Creative Thinking* (New York: Harper, 1986).

Eugene Raudsepp, *More Creative Growth Games* (New York: G. P. Putnam's Sons, 1980).

14

Vantage Points

Purpose

To show how viewing life from various perspectives fosters understanding of and empathy toward individuals' unique circumstances.

Materials Needed

Pencils, paper for all
White board or newsprint, marker

Preparation

An outline map of the United States should be drawn on the white board or newsprint. Also, cards for the Partial Pictures activity should be prepared.

Introduction

Several years ago, William Least Heat Moon set out on an incredible cross-country journey. Despondent over a job loss and recent divorce, the former college teacher and Sioux Indian decided that, in his words, "a man who couldn't make things go right could at least go." With his life savings of $428 tucked under the dashboard of his van, Moon left Missouri and took to the road.

He would cover over thirteen thousand miles of highway before his return. But the highways Moon chose to travel were not the main thoroughfares and interstates of this country. Instead, he chose the less-traveled highways for his adventure, roads that at certain times of the day actually took on a mysterious cast of blue. That singular feature would one day work to Moon's benefit. *Blue Highways* became the title of the best-selling book about his experiences on America's backroads.

Along the way Moon discovered such diverse places as Remote, Oregon; Nameless, Tennessee; New Freedom, Pennsylvania; Why, Arizona; and Whynot, Mississippi.

The people he met were also colorful. There was Bill Hammond, a boatbuilder; Alice Middleton, a former school teacher and now octogenarian; and Brother Patrick, a Trappist monk who used to be a patrolman. By being with them, Moon would come to know their stories.

Moon, on the final leg of his journey, has stopped at a service station. He writes,

> The pump attendant, looking at my license plate when he had filled the tank, asked, "Where you coming from, Show Me?"
> "Where I've been."
> "Where else?" he said.[1]

The author's journey taught him a great deal about his native land. But more importantly, because of where he'd been, he had shared in the essence of others' existence from their vantage point.

Bridge

Like William Least Heat Moon, where we have been can be a key to understanding others. Experiences, not geographical locations, enable us to view life from another's vantage point.

Trying to understand people can be frustrating. But our own experiences provide us with a reference point. Whether it be joy, suffering, turmoil, or peace, these places of our hearts are keys that can unlock the doors of empathy and understanding.

Just where have we been? Within this group alone journeys have been made to many different "life points." Some have been joy-filled jaunts, other treks have ended in places of distress. But wherever we have been, it can be encouraging just to know that someone has been there before us. Let's discover, in a nonthreatening way, some of the life-places we have been.

Activity: "States of Experience"

Distribute index cards and pencils to participants. Have group members write down a place (situation or experience) where they have experienced a significant life episode (joy, suffering). This should be creatively described in a one- or two-word place-name, followed by the name of one of the forty-eight states. Example: Great *Depression*, Wyoming. Explain clearly that the cards will be read aloud, but that they will first be shuffled to preserve anonymity. This will help individuals to decide how transparent they wish to be.

After a minute or two, have the members pass the index cards to the right. This continues until the leader calls out "Stop!" Participants keep the card they hold at that point.

Finally, ask for each person to tell the place described on his or her card. Write the appropriate spot on the U. S. map.

The primary purpose of "States of Experience" is to show that, even within the immediate group, individuals have passed through many different circumstances and experiences. A secondary benefit is the encouragement specific group members may receive simply by learning of others' past predicaments.

Bridge

A look at our map shows at least a few of the "states" we have been in: experiences that have shaped our lives.

Experience is a key ingredient in learning to see from another's vantage point. By referring to what we have experienced—where we have been—our chances of understanding another's perspective or behavior is increased.

When you have experienced destitution, you understand the humiliation that accompanies the offer of charity.

When you have experienced anorexia nervosa, you do not so easily discount a friend's obsession with thinness.

When you have experienced abuse, another's bruises become a matter of deep concern.

When you have experienced the struggle of alcoholism, you are more sure to affirm one who is fighting the same battle.

When you have experienced giving to those who have little, you resonate with those who live only to give.

And when you have experienced freedom in Christ, you celebrate more fully another's commitment.

Where we have been and what we have experienced allows us to view life from another's vantage point.

Biblical Perspective

There is no finer example of the life of experience than that of Jesus. Woven throughout the gospels are accounts of his involvement in others' lives.

Luke 19 captures Jesus taking advantage of an opportunity. The Savior has spotted Zacchaeus sitting in a sycamore tree. But Jesus is not content to leave the tax-man alone. Verse five begins, "When Jesus reached the spot, he looked up and said to him, 'Zacchaeus, come down immediately. I must stay at your house today.' So he came down at once and welcomed him gladly."

But the Master's bed and breakfast choice rankled the self-righteous. Verse seven: "All the people saw this and began to mutter, 'He has gone to be the the the guest of a 'sinner'.' "

Jesus, however, would not be deterred from the ensuing experience.

"But Zacchaeus stood up and said to the Lord, 'Look, Lord! Here and now I give half of my possessions to the poor, and if I have cheated anybody out of anything, I will pay back four times the amount.' "

You can almost hear the cheers in that crowded house of old. And then Jesus, with love in his voice and a glint in his eyes, affirms the decision, "Today salvation has come to this house . . ."

Zacchaeus had turned his heart toward heaven, and Jesus had been there to savor the experience.

Our Redeemer took many such highways and byways through-out his earthly existence. He calls us to go where he has been.

Bridge

Limited experience in life makes it more difficult to view life from another's vantage point. It is like living in a country without knowing the language. The end result is that we simply can't understand what is happening. But a broad base of life experience allows us to understand the most important vocabulary of all: the language of others' lives.

Of course, Jesus knew there would be circumstances when to experience another's situation, even for the sake of ministry, would be unwise. So it is for us today. We are not called to become drunkards to minister effectively to the alcoholic. The Savior knew where to draw the line between association as a friend, and participation in a source of struggle.

There is, however, something else that can help us reach out to those whose lives are being lived at places where we have never been. Where experience falls short, information can fill in.

Being informed on a variety of life issues is critical for the caring Christian. Ignorance helps no one. But learning what makes people tick can help us both detect and meet needs in the tradition of Jesus Christ.

The avenues of information are many; libraries, schools, seminars, and simply asking questions are just a few things that can help us learn to see from another's vantage point.

What kind of difference can being an informed Christian make? For one thing, it can help "fill in the blanks" of another's behavior or lifestyle. Here's how!

Activity: "Partial Pictures"

Write the following on the white board or newsprint:

Arenas of Understanding

Dynamics of grief
Single parenthood
Cultural differences
Perfectionism
Religious convictions

Write the following situations on separate index cards (or photocopy and cut into slips):

1. "I just don't understand Eleanor. Sure, losing a husband hurts. But she's so depressed. If I were her, I'd buck up and get on with my life."
2. "I've quit asking Roger to go anywhere with me. Ever since Laura left him and their son, for some reason all he can think about is work. I think he's trying to forget his pain by losing himself in his job."
3. "Could you believe it? I'll say this much—that's the last time we're going to invite a foreigner home from church for dinner. The outfit I could handle, but not his post-meal belching!"
4. "It's like the world has come to an end or something. Tracy gets a B in Physics and she comes unglued. 'It's the first time I've gotten a grade lower than an A,' she says. I say, what's the big deal; just forget it. Maybe it's time I found a new best friend. This one's driving me nuts!"
5. "So there we are, out of gas on a Pennsylvania back road. Well, I walk up to this white farmhouse, knock on the door, and a bearded guy wearing suspenders opens it. I ask him if I can buy a little gas from him, just enough to get me to the nearest town. Get this: he tells me he doesn't have any! Can you believe it? A farmer without even a little can of

gas? Well, right then I told him thanks for nothing and that I hoped everybody in Pennsylvania wasn't so unwilling to help out a stranger."

Narrator Bridges (for leader's use):

1. *"Ignorance* says Eleanor is a wimp. But *informed* on the dynamics of grief, you understand that . . ."
2. *"Ignorance* says Roger is suppressing his emotions and withdrawing. But *informed* on single-parenting you understand that . . ."
3. *"Ignorance* says the belcher belongs in a barnyard. But *informed* on cultural characteristics you understand that . . ."
4. *"Ignorance* says that a passing grade is enough. But *informed* on perfectionism you understand that . . ."
5. *"Ignorance* says the farmer is unfriendly. But *informed* on religious convictions you understand that . . ."

Write the following (or photocopy) clarification statements on another set of cards:

1A. Depression is an appropriate and expected dynamic in the experience of grief. Encouragement and support are what Eleanor needs, not insensitivity and a call to stoic demeanor.

2A. Raising a child on a single income gives work high-priority status in any single parent's life. And when Roger's not working, he knows that his son needs what time he has left. Single-parenting is tough, but Roger is making it. Affirmation should take the place of condemnation.

3A. In this man's country, an after-dinner belch is considered a compliment to the host. No, it probably isn't something you want to consider as a future family tradition. Simply view it as thank you from the bottom of an appreciative belly.

4A. For the perfectionist, anything less than the best is the worst. An emotional disorder, perfectionism cannot simply be turned off when disaster strikes. Tracy needs to be shown through unconditional love and acceptance, not rejection, that her personhood is not dependent on a perfect performance.

5A. The Amish, many of whom live in Pennsylvania, opt for a simple lifestyle. Their religious beliefs lead many of them to reject modern conveniences such as automobiles, power machinery, electricity, individual telephones, and other entities thought to be too worldly. Obviously, gasoline finds little meaning on a farm which does not require it. Far from unfriendly, the typical Amish person is, however, committed to his faith.

Here's how the activity works. Explain that a perspective emanating from a position of ignorance will be read aloud. You will then bridge the perspective to a position of being informed, pointing to the "Arena of Understanding" which can help clarify the true situation. Finally, the individual with the corresponding card will read his or her clarification statement aloud.

Example

1. First participant reads *Perspective* card #1 aloud.
2. Narrator refers to Arena of Understanding "Dynamics of Grief," then reads *Narrator Bridge* #1 aloud.
3. Second participant reads *Clarification* card #1A aloud.

Follow this succession for each of the remaining cards.

"Partial Pictures" shows how being an informed Christian can give us the perspective we need to more fully understand others.

Wrap-up

In 1959, John Howard Griffin, a caucasian, had his skin cosmetically changed to resemble that of a black person. Griffin then went to live as a black man in the southern United States. His book, *Black Like Me,* tells of the prejudice he came to know as a result of his undercover work.

As Griffin learned, viewing life from another's perspective can produce pain. But sometimes an uncomfortable position is the most valuable vantage point. When we know how another is hurting, we are better prepared for the task of healing. Perhaps that is the most pointed advantage of learning to see from another's vantage point.

Discussion Questions

1. What is the ultimate purpose of learning to see from another's vantage point?
2. Besides Zacchaeus, what are some other examples of Jesus' experiencing the dynamics of others' situations?
3. Does a time ever come when attempting to understand another's point of view becomes a worthless endeavor? If so, when?
4. Several arenas of understanding were mentioned in this program (cultural, religious). What are some others? Which is the most difficult to grasp?
5. Understanding another's point of view can sometimes happen most effectively in a forum specifically designed to accomplish that purpose, such as contract negotiations. What basic principles from these kinds of corporate experiences can be applied to our personal quests for understanding?

Suggested Scripture

Psalm 8:1–5; John 11:32–35; Hebrews 4:15–16.

For Further Reading

John Griffin, *Black Like Me* (Boston, Mass. Houghton Mifflin, 1960).

William Least Heat Moon, *Blue Highways* (New York: Fawcett Crest, 1982).

15

Worship While You Work

Purpose

To consider work as a God-given entity, and thereby affirm its inherent dignity.

Materials Needed

Paper, pencils for all
Hat or basket

Activity: "Jumbled Jobs"

As an icebreaker have participants write their occupations in scrambled form on sheets of paper. For example, a secretary might write "ecrtysear." (If a participant is not currently working, ask the same question regarding whatever he or she is primarily occupied with throughout an average day. Also, students may wish to write the occupation they'd like to have when they finish school.)

Collect the slips in a hat or basket. Group members then each draw one paper, attempt to decode it, and locate the individual to whom it belongs. Instruct participants to ask that person to answer two questions: what is the thing you like most about your job, and what is the thing you like least about your job?

After a couple of minutes, regroup and solicit at random how various individual's partners responded.

"Jumbled Jobs" is designed to both create a relaxed atmosphere and direct attention to the topic of work.

Introduction

Work has many meanings. Some find deep joy and satisfaction in it. But others may consider work a "necessary evil," an unavoidable means to an end called existence. For some, work is merely an avenue to play. The paycheck will fill with thrills until Monday; then the cycle starts all over again. To still others, work becomes an escape from domestic problems.

Many find satisfaction in the workplace but much of the world finds it less than fulfilling. Many share Mark Twain's view: "I do not like work even when someone else does it."

We live in a world which revolves around work; how would God have us relate to it? A quiz may help answer that question!

Activity: "Work Wise"

Distribute pencils and paper to group members. Then ask the following questions aloud, allowing ample time for participants to write responses:

1. True or false: The primary objective of work is to make money.
2. Work is primarily a result of (a) the fall in Eden, (b) personal choice in the here and now, (c) societal expectations, (d) none of the above, or (e) all of the above.
3. True or false: *Occupation* and *vocation* are two words which describe the same thing.
4. Fill-in-the-blank: For the Christian, potential for _____ in the workplace should be of primary concern.
5. A job loss may threaten an individual most because of the corresponding loss of (a) feelings of accomplishment, (b) community status, (c) self-identity, or (d) self-worth.
6. True or false: Work is of more value than leisure.

7. Agree/disagree: "Those who work much do not work hard" (Henry David Thoreau).
8. Fill in the blank: _____ is the key ingredient in job satisfaction.
9. Christian commitment demands pursuing employment based primarily on (a) marketplace needs, (b) God-given abilities, (c) witnessing opportunities, (d) personal goals, or (e) other.
10. True or false: Overall, the Protestant work ethic has been more of a help than a hindrance in fostering a balanced view of work.

Discussion

After the quiz, have group members "correct" their work. Ask respondents to raise their hands according to their answers. While most of the questions will have been answered somewhat subjectively, use the following to foster deeper discussion:

For question:

1. ("The primary objective of work is to make money.") Questions: If this is true, why? If false, what should the primary objective be? Can the average worker's primary objective be anything other than monetary compensation? Would a third-world worker answer differently?
2. ("Work is primarily a result of (a) the fall in Eden, (b) personal choices in the here and now, (c) societal expectations, (d) all of the above, or (e) none of the above.") The biblical record suggests that *"e," none of the above,* would be the appropriate response. The curse following the entrance of sin into the world merely introduced the elements of difficulty and struggle into human labor. (See Gen. 3:17.) According to Genesis 1:28, Adam and Eve were assigned the task of "managing" God's creation from the beginning. Question: What might have been the purpose of work prior to the fall?

3. *("Occupation* and *vocation* are two words which describe the same thing.") While both words can relate to work, the word *vocation* comes from a word meaning "a calling." Could a person's occupation be different than his vocation? Why/why not?

4. ("For the Christian, potential for _____ in the workplace should be of primary concern.") Discuss options, which might include: advancement, ministry/witnessing, personal growth, professional growth, increased income. Question: Is the pursuit of any of these wrong?

5. ("A job loss may threaten an individual most because of the corresponding loss of (a) feelings of accomplishment, (b) community status, (c) self-identity, (d) self-worth.") Both (c) and or (d) would probably be root issues for someone experiencing a job loss. Self-identity in particular can be shaken, as one's entire existence often evolves around his or her work. Questions: Is having one's self-identity so closely tied to work a healthy thing? How can a person appropriately disassociate oneself from work?

6. ("Work is of more value than leisure.") Tim Hansel points out that the Latin word for *leisure* was *licere,* which means "to be permitted." The Latin word for *work* on the other hand, was *negotium,* which is translated "nonleisure." In other words, as they are related to each other work was actually secondary to leisure. Hansel also points out that the Greek word for leisure was *ascholia,* which leads to the English word for *school.* In the Greek world, leisure was a time for learning.[1] Question: Given the aforementioned definition of leisure, what are some ways that a Christian might spend genuine "leisure time"?

7. ("Agree/disagree: 'Those who work much do not work hard' " [Henry David Thoreau]) Question: What do you think Thoreau was suggesting by this statement? If you agreed, why? If not, why not?

8. ("Fill in the blank: '_____ is the key ingredient in job satisfaction.' ") Question: Would this key likely be different for the Christian and non-Christian? If so, in what way/s?

9. ("Christian commitment demands pursuing employment based primarily on (a) marketplace needs, (b) God-given abilities, (c) witnessing opportunities, (d) personal goals, (e) other.") The criteria for landing a job may be more complex than one "primary" consideration. Ask for respondents to tell why they answered as they did, particularly those who selected "other." Question: Should job-hunting be geared around our own or others' needs? In what way/s?

10. ("True or false: Overall, the Protestant work ethic has been more of a help than a hindrance in fostering a balanced view of work.") The Protestant work ethic basically suggests that work is of God, and as such should be embraced with zeal and diligence. Question: If true, in what ways has this perspective been helpful? If false, how has it been harmful?

Bridge

No amount of discussion can change one fact—our work is still with us. To discover how our work can work for us, let's look at the Good Book!

Biblical Perspective

There is no question that we are called to live responsibly. This involves work as the apostle Paul states in 1 Thessalonians 4:11–12: "Make it your ambition to lead a quiet life, to mind your own business and to work with your hands, just as we told you, so that your daily life may win the respect of outsiders and so that you will not be dependent on anybody."

Paul is even more direct in 2 Thessalonians 3:10, "If a man will not work, he shall not eat."

But the biblical call to work is not a summons to misery. The Book of Ecclesiastes sets forth a valuable perspective on work. In the third chapter, beginning with verse 12, the author writes: "I know that there is nothing better for men than to be happy and do good while they live. That every man may eat and drink, and find satisfaction in all his toil—this is the gift of God."

Here is the scriptural balance then: to work, but to whenever possible enjoy that same work, knowing that it is a gift of God. Because work is heaven-sent there is inherent dignity. From homework to housework to every legitimate work, none is menial in the eyes of God. True, not all employment is fun. A fulfilling job is ideal, indeed to be pursued.

Nevertheless, reality in the workplace can sometimes be less-than-heavenly. But as Christians, whatever our occupation, we are through our jobs doing the work of Christ on earth. Not merely as his witnesses, but as living tools used of him to accomplish his sovereign will. How? Doug Sherman describes one way in his book *Your Work Matters to God.* He writes,

> A friend of mine operates a pallet company. Pallets are the platforms used extensively in the transportation industries, designed to make it easier for forklifts to load and unload stacks of goods. My friend's company manufactures these pallets.
>
> Now, how could my friend's pallets possibly fit into the work of God in the world? Actually, they are an important, albeit humble link in a complex chain that God uses to meet my needs and your needs. Those pallets are an indispensable part of the trucking industry—an industry that delivers ruby-red grapefruit from the Rio Grande, boxes of cereal from Battle Creek, Michigan, and milk from Coppell, Texas, to a supermarket near my home.
>
> All of these come together at my family's breakfast table. Before we eat, one of my children thanks God for the food. Why? Because He has brought to our table something we need.
>
> . . . did you notice my friend's pallets? They were tucked away under those crates of grapefruit, boxes of cereal, and gallons of milk. Though obscure, God used them to meet my family's needs."[2]

In large, small, and sometimes even unseen ways, each of his children contributes to the uplifting of humanity through his or her job. Knowing that, we can tackle our tasks with joy, even amid the curse of toil. By offering our best efforts back to God, our work stations become places of worship.

Wrap-up

Someday, we will live without labor unions. It seems unlikely, however, that work, a responsible return of our abilities to God, will be a thing of the past. The curse will indeed be lifted in heaven. But knowing God more deeply will likely continue to happen in myriad ways, including through the fruits of our labors. From plants grown under our care to the study of the universe, the pursuit of understanding God will go on. Happily, such "work" will be nothing short of sheer pleasure.

For Discussion Questions, see activity "Job Wise."

Suggested Scripture

Genesis 1:26, 28–29, 2:15; Ecclesiastes 3:12, 5:18; 1 Thessalonians 4:11–12.

For Further Reading

Garry Friesen, *Decision Making and the Will of God* (Portland: Multnomah Press: 1983).

Doug Sherman and William Hendricks, *Your Work Matters to God* (Colorado Springs: NavPress, 1988).

16

Mixers

Mixers are short activities designed to help foster an atmosphere of warmth, acceptance, and equality in your meeting. They also provide group members the opportunity to learn new things about each other.

Try one of these mixers at the beginning of your next gathering. Along with completing the specific task for each mixer, regular attendees should introduce themselves to newcomers and make them feel welcome.

1. Participants greet all other individuals whose birthday is during the same month as their own. If someone is present who does not share a birthday month with another person, all group members converge on that individual with words and gestures of welcome!

2. Count the group off by fours. Same-numbers tell each other an important "discovery" made during the past week.

3. Allow two minutes for individuals to learn the favorite foods of others in the group. The person able to recall the most, along with whose favorite each item was, receives a food prize (cookie, cupcake, brownie).

4. Participants shake hands and greet as many people as possible whom they haven't seen since the last meeting.

5. Count off the group using the following designations: (1) Boat, (2) Plane, (3) Car, and (4) Train. Same-designation

persons greet each other, then tell their favorite place to visit.

6. Participants greet five others in the room using (in sequence) the following one word greetings: (1) "So" (2) "nice" (3) "to" (4) "see" (5) "you." The last person greeted by each person is to tell a highlight from their past week.

7. Count the group off using the following categories: (1) Cover, (2) Title, (3) Page, and (4) Index. Members of individual categories greet each other, then tell an insight or other highlight gleaned from a recently-read book or article.

8. Group members choose one other person with whom to tell the information requested in the first "round" of this experience. Whenever the words "Dooka, Dooka," are called out by the leader, they must supply the information requested by the leader to each other. When the leader calls out the words "Dooka, Dooka" again, each person must quickly locate another person to continue the exercise with, awaiting the next question from the leader. Following are some "Dooka, Dooka" questions (allow 30 seconds for each question to be responded to):

   If you could live anywhere in the world, where would it be, and why?

   Who is a particularly intriguing historical character to you, and why?

   What is your favorite Bible story or verse?

9. The group forms a circle, and the leader takes a "Scepter of Friendship" (this can be any item, or a specially-designated object) in hand. The leader hands the scepter to a group member, and addresses this individual with brief words of welcome, encouragement, affirmation, etc. This person then transfers the scepter to another person, and the process continues until all group members have participated.

10. Participants write a little-known fact about themselves on 3 X 5 cards. The cards are mixed and distributed at random (make sure nobody receives their own card). Each card is in turn read aloud, and the writer identifies himself or her-

self. (If desired, allow participants to guess the writer's identity.)

11. Have a group member say a number between one and nine. Ask another person to locate that digit on his or her social security number, and read it aloud. Participants shake the hands of that many group members. If the digit is below two, specify another digit to be read and combine the two numbers. This can also be used with telephone and driver's license numbers, etc.

12. The group stands and forms a "circle of friendship." Participants go around the circle, telling either a high or low point of their week. Finally, the leader reads (1) a Scripture passage of praise and thanksgiving and (2) a passage of encouragement.

13. Each participant tells three others in the group a country, state, or city/town where he or she has lived prior to the current place of residence, and something missed about the former residence. If someone has never lived elsewhere, have that person share something enjoyable about that fact.

14. Count the group off according to the following categories: (1) Here's (2) What, (3) I, and (4) Remember. Members of individual categories tell where they were when they learned of a significant world event, and what that event was (i.e., attempt on Reagan's life, war in the Persian Gulf, etc.)

15. Place random letters of the alphabet in separate envelopes, one letter per envelope. Distribute the envelopes to group members, and have them form a circle. After opening the envelope, group members in turn greet the individual to the right, using the letter received to begin the first word of that greeting. For example, a person with the letter B might say, "Begin having a great day right now!" Tip: Use letters that will not be too difficult to work with: A, D, S, T.

These are just a few ideas for mixers. Encourage group members to create simple, fun, meaningful mixers of their own.

Endnotes

Chapter 2

1. Gordon MacDonald, *Ordering Your Private World* (Nashville: Thomas Nelson, 1984), p. 117.

2. Adapted from Lewis Timberlake, *It's Always Too Soon to Quit* (Old Tappan, N. J.: Revell, (1988), pp. 45–47.

Chapter 3

1. Jon Johnston, *Christian Excellence: Alternative to Success* (Grand Rapids: Baker Book House, 1985), p. 33.

Chapter 4

1. Bruce Narramore, *You're Someone Special* (Grand Rapids: Zondervan, 1978), p. 61.

2. S. Rickly Christian, *Alive!* (Wheaton, Ill.: Tyndale House, 1983), p. 35.

3. An optional feature presentation that complements this program is the skit "What's Les Worth?" found in *Creative Skits for Youth Groups 2* (Grand Rapids: Baker Book House, 1989).

Chapter 5

1. "The Case of the Baker Street Plans," *Reader's Digest,* March 1950, pp. 49–50 (condensed from *The Baker Street Journal*).

2. Ibid.

3. *The Interpreter's Bible,* vol. XII (New York, Abingdon Press, 1957) p. 40.

Chapter 6

1. Jerry and Mary White, *Friends and Friendship: The Secrets of Drawing Closer* (Colorado Springs, NavPress, 1982), p. 10.

2. An effective addition to the wrap-up is to play the song "Special Friend" by Christine Wyrtzen (Milk 'n Honey Records, 1980).

3. Script taken from 1 Samuel 20, New English Bible (Cambridge University Press, 1961).

Chapter 7

1. Joni Eareckson–Tada, *Choices, Changes* (Grand Rapids: Zondervan, 1986), p. 35.

Chapter 8

1. Anthony Campolo, *Who Switched the Price Tags?* (Waco, Tex.: Word, 1987), p. 28, 29.

2. Elisabeth Elliot, *Through Gates of Splendor* (New York: Harper, 1957). The story is reconstructed from the book.

3. Over the years some progress has been made in reaching the Aucas. This story, however, is intended to focus more on the decision-making process of the martyrs than on the results of their risk.

4. *Gates*, p. 176.

Chapter 9

1. A good resource is *The New American Dictionary of First Names* (New York: New American Library, 1983).

2. William Dyrness, *Themes in Old Testament Theology* (Downers Grove, Ill.: Inter-Varsity, 1979), p. 45.

3. Ibid., pp. 45–47.

4. R. C. Sproul, *The Holiness of God* (Wheaton, Ill.: Tyndale, 1985), p. 148.

5. For more on this subject see *The God Who Hears* by W. Bingham Hunter, chapter 15, "Concluding: What's in Jesus' Name?" (Inter-Varsity Press, 1986).

Chapter 11

1. Norman Geisler, *Options in Contemporary Christian Ethics* (Grand Rapids: Baker, 1981).
2. Ibid., p. 87.
3. Ibid., p. 109.
4. Ibid., pp. 92, 93.
5. Ibid., p. 110.

Chapter 12

1. W. Bingham Hunter in *The God Who Hears,* quoting from Lewis Carroll's *Through the Looking Glass* in *The Annotated Alice* (New York: Clarkson H. Potter, 1960), p. 251.
2. C. S. Lewis, *Mere Christianity* (New York: Macmillan, 1943), p. 123.
3. From *Faith Passages and Patterns* by Thomas A. Droege (Philadelphia: Fortress Press, 1983), ch. 3, "Faith Seeking Understanding," pp. 45–63.

Chapter 13

1. Sue Monk Kidd, *Discipleship Journal*, "Living on the Creative Edge," Issue 48.
2. Tim Stafford, *Knowing the Face of God* (Grand Rapids: Zondervan, 1986), p. 197.
3. Ibid., p. 177.

Chapter 14

1. William Least Heat Moon, *Blue Highways* (New York: Fawcett Crest, 1982), p. 426.

Chapter 15

1. Tim Hansel, *When I Relax I Feel Guilty* (Elgin, Ill.: David C. Cook, 1979), p. 30.
2. Doug Sherman and William Hendricks, *Your Work Matters to God* (Colorado Springs: NavPress, 1988), p. 89.